100156457 X

TELEPEN

189876

TEACHING CHILDREN WITH SEVERE LEARNING DIFFICULTIES: A RADICAL REAPPRAISAL

12. DEC

D1344318

CROOM HELM SERIES ON SPECIAL EDUCATIONAL
NEEDS: POLICY, PRACTICES AND SOCIAL ISSUES

General Editor: Len Barton, Westhill College,
Birmingham

SPECIAL EDUCATION AND SOCIAL INTERESTS
Edited by Len Barton and Sally Tomlinson

COPING WITH SPECIAL NEEDS:
A Guide for New Teachers
Geof Sewell

REDEFINING REMEDIAL EDUCATION
Hazel Bines

TEACHING CHILDREN WITH SEVERE LEARNING DIFFICULTIES
A Radical Reappraisal

SUE WOOD AND BARBARA SHEARS

SHEFFIELD HALLAM UNIVERSITY
LEARNING CENTRE
WITHDRAWN FROM STOCK

CROOM HELM
London • Sydney • Wolfeboro, New Hampshire

© 1986 Sue Wood and Barbara Shears
Croom Helm Ltd, Provident House, Burrell Row,
Beckenham, Kent, BR3 1AT

Croom Helm Australia Pty Ltd, Suite 4, 6th Floor,
64-76 Kippax Street, Surry Hills, NSW 2010, Australia

British Library Cataloguing in Publication Data

Wood, Sue
    Teaching children with severe learning
    difficulties: a radical reappraisal.
    1. Learning disabilities
    I. Title II. Shears, Barbara
    371.9'043 LC4704

    ISBN 0-7099-3682-6
    ISBN 0-7099-3690-7 Pbk

Croom Helm, 27 South Main Street,
Wolfeboro, New Hampshire 03894-2069, USA

Library of Congress Cataloging in Publication Data
applied for:

level 4

SHEFFIELD CITY POLYTECHNIC LIBRARY

371.9043
WO

COLLEGIATE CRESCENT

Printed and bound in Great Britain
by Billing & Sons Limited, Worcester.

CONTENTS

Contents

ACKNOWLEDGEMENTS

We would like to express our appreciation and sincere thanks to both family and close friends for their support, advice and patience throughout the many stages of the writing of this book.

We are grateful to our anonymous referee for constructive criticism, and to Len Barton for his faith in us.

Our thanks also go to those who have typed the many scripts.

The views expressed throughout the book are our own and do not necessarily reflect those of our employers.

"Unless you believe that people are people
regardless of their abilities or disabilities
and that they can do what they really want to
do, you will impose limitations on them"
(Williams and Shoultz, 1982, p. 124).

SERIES EDITORS' INTRODUCTION

With the advent of the Warnock Report and the more
recent introduction and growing implementation of
the 1981 Education Act, schools face new challenges
relating to the identification and provision of
increasing numbers of pupils with special educational needs. The position of the teacher in this
process, her skills and commitment, is given a
place of prominence in both official documents and
other literature dealing with the question of the
education of these children. Teachers are viewed
as key workers through whom policy needs to be
implemented and expectations satisfied.

This book emphasises the importance of a
reflexive pedagogy, one in which teachers, both
collectively and individually, seriously examine
the underlying assumptions and value judgements
that permeate policy and practice within schools.
The authors wish to encourage debate and analysis
over the question of the rights and educational
experiences of children with severe learning
difficulties. The writers forcibly remind us that,
in relation to this group of pupils, there exists
an unacceptable gulf between laudible rhetoric and
the realities of discriminatory policy and
practice. By challenging some of the assumptions
involved in the dominant orthodoxy within the
literature dealing with the education of these
children, value is placed upon alternative ways of
thinking and working. Nor do the authors
underestimate the difficulties in attempting to
contribute to the realisation of such change,
particularly if there is to be a move beyond
cosmetic or piecemeal change. What they do
acknowledge is that teachers need both the
encouragement and opportunity to discuss with
colleagues issues facing them in particular

situations. This will be absolutely essential for effective action to be marshalled through, for example, the medium of whole school policies.

The writers argue for the centrality of social and situational factors in the construction of handicap. These include issues of ideology, expectations, curriculum and the institutionalised nature of school life. Through this means a series of challenging questions are raised that cover such such topics as:

What constitutes good teaching?
To what extent do the interactions between teachers and pupils provide a means of enhancing pupil self esteem?
How far does the curriculum recognise existing abilities and provide a means of enhancing cooperative learning?
Will the development of a self advocacy movement increase the possibilities for change?

Although the intention of the writers is to contribute to an examination of existing practices, by being concerned with the rights of pupils and the quality of their experiences, the overall impact of the book is to raise the seriously underexamined question of the future role of special schools.

The analysis offered in this book has been informed by the authors' varied experiences as students, teachers and through insights derived from interactions with other colleagues. They use this valuable resource to interrogate ideas and to attempt to unpack some of the complex issues involved in the relationship between schools and society, and teachers and pupils. They do not attempt to offer slick, easy answers and they recognise that future developments remain uncertain, but this book does provide stimulus for thought and will, hopefully, contribute to further debate, as well as encouraging alternative ways of working.

Len Barton
Bristol

INTRODUCTION

Since the 1970 Education Act which brought severely
mentally handicapped children into the state education system, educationalists have looked to the
development of a special curriculum suited to the
education of these children, as distinct from their
training.   The objectives model was enthusiastic-
ally embraced early on as providing for education
(Cunningham 1974; McMaster 1973; Gunzberg 1974b;
Kiernan 1974). Within this model aims and objectives were arranged hierarchically, the latter
being subordinate to the former, expressing the
conception of education as a means to prespecified
ends. Those ends were usually referred to in terms
of developing the full potential of individuals and
teaching them to be as independent as they were
capable of.
        Since the early 1970s, the necessity for
teachers   of   children   with   severe   learning
difficulties to plan exactly what they were
proposing to teach, in the form of precise
objectives of pupil outcomes, defined in small
incremental steps, has been frequently reiterated
both by authorities in the field and in official
documents. That the child with severe learning
difficulties has a need for this style of education
is now taken as virtually a self evident truth.
Neither is the question as to what objectives
should be geared towards seen as problematic, since
the inclusion of severely subnormal children in the
education system has been taken to mean that the
aims of education and its purpose are universal.
The aims of education for all children are now
defined in terms of personal development and
development for independence and community living.
According to this general viewpoint children only
differ in terms of how far along the road to

1

achieving the aims of education they can get, given specialised support and help (i.e. special educational provision). In the practice of education for children with severe learning difficulties, teaching for independence is taken to subsume personal development and is seen as an activity necessarily prior to community living. That objectives should determine functional skills, i.e. those of direct use within these aims, has become to be accepted in England during the last decade or so.

The curriculum which has been produced has ostensibly dealt with the issues raised during the 1970s and early 1980s with regard to what education for children with severe learning difficulties should be about and what represented good practice. It is special, i.e. different from mainstream curricula; it lays out specific guidelines for the generation of aims, objectives and teaching methodology and therefore gives guidance as to what and how to teach and what passes for education; it produces precise, clear objectives so that teachers may know precisely what it is they are or should be teaching; it makes the teacher more accountable because of the structures imposed and the requirement of recording programmes, and because checks can be made on whether objectives have been achieved; it allows for parent-teacher collaboration in working towards specific objectives; it allows for direct relevance to the special needs of individual children since what is to be taught is seen in relation to what the child can/can't do already, in a very precise manner; it involves individual programme planning, therefore catering for the heterogeneity of mentally handicapped children; and it provides for continuous assessment and evaluation directly linked to teaching.

It is tacitly assumed that the programmes generated by this curriculum model, within the skills analysis paradigm, represent education and that as such, education for children with severe learning difficulties is outside of the medical model of handicap, where handicap is seen as pathological and denotes the need for a specific type of treatment based on the type of handicap, i.e. management, environment, handling, and training of a very different kind to other people.

The 1981 Education Act embodies the rhetoric of special education as education geared to individual needs rather than special educational treat-

ment as a response to types of handicaps and therefore particular types of special educational provision. Special education is therefore put forward
as a response to the individual, not his condition.
For children with severe learning difficulties the
subsequent recommendations and circulars have adopted the objectives model within the skills analysis
paradigm in a way in which it is apparent that this
approach is being taken to represent <u>the</u> means of
educating these children.

However, the new orthodox curriculum for
children with severe learning difficulties is
defined in narrow terms using a normative perspective which places formal and functional skills in
an illusionary position as a passport to participation and acceptance in the dominant living patterns
and culture of mainstream society. It purports the
false logic that acquisition of discrete skills
will enable mentally handicapped adults to be as
independent as possible. In so doing, the social,
economic and political factors involved in the
classification of mental handicap and in creating
and maintaining handicapping conditions, are discounted.

Educational practice which aims to normalise
children with severe learning difficulties, i.e.
make them more normal, devalues them in terms of
the people they actually are. It creates handicap
itself. Present trends - to use behavioural objectives and teach discrete skills - treat children
with severe learning difficulties as objects.
Assessment and teaching do not make any significant
allowances for children to have perspectives of
their own which may differ from the mainstream view
about what is desirable and necessary. Within the
educational context, children with severe learning
difficulties are not seen as children who have
minds of their own, but as malfunctioning systems.
The analogy of a car with a 'weak engine' chosen by
the staff of Rectory Paddock School to explain the
supposed need for the curriculum to 'identify key
points of weakness.....make concentrated efforts to
analyse and remedy as many of those weaknesses as
possible' (Staff of Rectory Paddock School 1981
p.9) exemplifies this view. The comparative success or failure of children with severe learning
difficulties within this view of education is not
only imputed to the degree of <u>their</u> <u>handicap</u> but
is also used as a definition of it. This means
that they are constantly devalued as mentally handicapped children because of their obvious

failure in comparison to the norm.

We came to write this book as a result of our own efforts as teachers to understand what was happening to ourselves, our colleagues and children with severe learning difficulties in special schools. From our experience as teachers we felt that both traditional ways of teaching and using popular behaviour modification techniques were not constructive ways of working with the children with whom we were concerned. Furthermore, we felt that the difficulties with which we were faced in terms of teaching and the methodology available to us, raised serious questions of ethics, as well as leading us to wonder what education was, or should be anyway. The issues we have raised in the book are precisely about these questions. They are concerned with opening up the debate about what constitutes education for children with severe learning difficulties and what, therefore, teaching is, should, might or could be about. We were faced with trying to 'teach' children who apparently refused to cooperate, showed no obvious interest in what we had to offer and in effect wanted very little to do with us. Instead they appeared to prefer to continue their own obsessive activities, and either withdrew or reacted violently when we tried to intervene in the ways suggested by most of the literature, by other professionals and 'experts' (notably educational psychologists). In these circumstances fundamental issues became more and more obvious to us as well as more and more of a concern. This led us to engage in critical analysis of not just what we were doing ourselves, but also of what was going on all around us. We felt there was such a level of taken for granted-ness in the education of children with severe learning difficulties, that basic assumptions concerning people's humanity and the respect due to both teachers and pupils as human beings and their rights as people were never consciously considered either as questions or issues. Any idea of what teachers were doing in the name of education being open to critical examination and question by their colleagues was similarly absent, or else viewed as 'unprofessional'.

This book is the result therefore of many years of questioning on our part. It is primarily addressed to teachers who are presently engaged in working with children with severe learning difficulties and to those in training or in other spheres of education who might wish to do so in the future. We hope too that it will be read by other professionals, administrators and politicians dealing with special education. It is aiming to challenge taken for granted beliefs and lay bare implicit assumptions and value judgements and thereby, we hope, provoke thought and generate debate. If we make even a few people uncomfortable in their familiar thought patterns and actions towards those they see as mentally handicapped and children with severe learning difficulties, we will have achieved our purpose in writing this book. Having said this however, we feel that the issues we have raised have very serious implications for any teacher and for the whole process of education in all schools.

A major theme throughout the book is the construction and effects of handicapping conditions for children with severe learning difficulties. Over the last 20 - 30 years there has been a growing recognition in the provision of services for people with special needs, of the distinctions that can be made between impairment, disability and handicap, and of the part social factors play in creating handicap. For example in 1980 the World Health Organisation issued its 'International Classification of Impairments, Disabilities and Handicaps' (in Heron and Myers 1983), defining the three terms in the following way: impairment as any loss or abnormality of psychological, physiological or anatomical structure or function; disability as the restriction or lack of ability to perform an activity resulting from an impairment; and handicap as the disadvantage for an individual that limits or prevents the fulfillment of a role that is 'normal'. It is clear that social factors directly contribute to creating and maintaining conditions which are handicapping to people with particular impairments through direct discrimination and as a result of dominant public and professional perceptions. Redressing the balance has been predominantly viewed in terms of freeing access, as in providing facilities for disabled people in public places such as ramps, or lifts, and in terms of policies of 'integration' and 'community care'.

Children with severe learning difficulties and mentally handicapped people are directly discriminated against by the lack of access for them to services, facilities and activities which the rest of us take for granted; by the provision of services for them in segregated settings; and by provision which is not of an equitable nature or

status to that provided for their peers. These
factors in themselves create handicapping
conditions, as does the granting of additional
supports, as if they were special privileges which
made up for lacking in other public and personal
domains and which are linked to dominant perceptions of children with severe learning difficulties
and mentally handicapped people as unable, incompetent, to be pitied. Handicapping conditions have
direct consequences for those concerned in terms of
limiting opportunities and conferring a particular
status. Their disability is seen as a negative
attribute and they are positioned as second class
citizens on the periphery of things, recipients of
social services and schooling, not producers and
consumers within society. The effect of handicapping conditions is to feed back into perceptions
of children with severe learning difficulties and
mentally handicapped people, reinforcing attitudes
and present discriminatory practices and legitimating them.

Integration of handicapped children into ordinary schools is put forward as a means to end the
discrimination involved in providing special education in segregated settings, and the 1981 Education
Act has to some extent embodied ideas about trying
to prevent the negative consequences of discrimination. We do not specifically address ourselves to
the issue of integration here, since the issues
raised in this book about the education of children
with severe learning difficulties have to be faced
whether or not these children are placed in integrated settings, because of the extent and nature of
the handicapping conditions they are subject to.
Integration in itself would not significantly alter
dominant perceptions of children with severe learning difficulties as mentally handicapped and the
kind of educational experiences they are subjected
to once in school, especially in the present circumstances where there is no likelihood of the
massive input of resources needed if they are actually to be taught alongside their ordinary peers
instead of in special units or classes. Therefore
this book is also a response to the 1981 Education
Act and to the current preoccupation with the question of integration, in terms of trying to make
explicit the complexity of handicapping conditions
and the fundamental nature of issues which teachers
must themselves address if they are to circumvent
disability and ameliorate the handicapping conditions which are socially constructed in peoples

everyday interactions with children with severe learning difficulties.

Terminology can itself be handicapping to people with disabilities because of the barriers labels erect to perceiving people as individuals with the same basic rights and needs as others. Instead labels like severe learning difficulty and mental handicap suggest that the people so categorised are fundamentally different from others, their disability being their defining characteristic. We wholeheartedly agree with the World Health Organisation's (WHO) categorisation of impairment, disability and handicap. We consequently found it extremely difficult to decide what terminology to use in the book. We have taken a pragmatic way out by using the terminology of the time, and referring to people with mental handicaps (rather than mentally handicapped people) where this seemed appropriate. The phraseology of people with intellectual impairments or learning disabilities seems more accurate and less derisory, but we have not used these terms since we feel it is more appropriate to wait for people with mental handicaps to decide for themselves how they wish to be referred to. Through the self advocacy movement 'people with mental handicaps' has been suggested to emphasise the idea that they are people first, and should be respected as such. We look forward to hearing more from them on this subject in the future.

Chapter One

THE SAGA OF CURRICULUM INNOVATION

There are now numerous publications which show how to go about choosing core curriculum areas, defining targets and assessing progress for children with severe learning difficulties. Most either explicitly or implicitly suggest a particular content which is thought congruent with a highly structured approach and the general aims of education. Furthermore, a certain teaching methodology ('precision teaching') tends to be referred to which explains getting from setting objectives to evaluating progress, i.e. actual learning and teaching (Kiernan et al. 1978; Kiernan 1981; Whelan and Speake 1979; Gardner et al. 1983). Articles about the skills analysis and objectives approach abound in all the relevant journals and magazines, not to mention the large number of American publications available in this country, many of which include complete inventories of skills to be taught and their components (e.g. Bender and Valletutti 1976; Snell 1978). Many schools all over the country have also produced, or are in the process of producing, their own 'core' curriculum along the lines sketched above, although few schools have had their work formally published.
          We do not mean to suggest that all or even many schools run the same educational programme for children with severe learning difficulties within their classrooms. In our experience schools differ widely in the depth of detail and specification which they have included in curriculum statements and in the way teachers make use of such curriculum statements for the generation of educational programmes for the group of children they are teaching. What we are concerned about are the distinctive trends emerging both in actual teaching practice across the country and in what teachers

8

are being given in terms of recommendations and judgements about what constitutes good teaching for children with severe learning difficulties. It is to these trends that we want to draw attention, as they represent particular aspects of what is now generally considered should make up the curriculum and the educational programme within this part of the special education system. As such, a new orthodoxy has emerged.

Since 1971 when mentally handicapped children officially became 'educable', the situation has changed from one in which there was a dearth of curriculum planning and development (Hughes 1975; Cunningham 1974), to one in which curriculum development workshops and information proliferate. Whereas in the early 1970s the curriculum in the then ESN(S) schools seemed to be viewed by teachers very much in terms of activities offered and the timetable (Hughes 1975; Leeming et al. 1979), aims, objectives and targets are now very much the order of the day. Previously, the idea that the educational programme for children with severe learning difficulties would consist of a watered down version of activities and tasks offered to mainstream infants did not necessarily seem too amiss, given the pupils' 'mental ages'. Nowadays making the comment that special education means simply getting the same education as usual but until you are much older, tends to denote a particular view of the special education system, rather than a commonly accepted definition of what goes on.

The development of a highly systematic and structured approach to the curriculum based on behavioural objectives and skills analysis, was premised by research evidence suggesting that mental handicap had certain characteristics which necessitated such a programme if progress was going to be made. At the same time, research was being published which showed that behavioural analysis and its concomitant techniques were successful, both in getting rid of 'problem' behaviours and in teaching new skills - to even the most profoundly handicapped child or adult (Whaley and Malott 1971; Ashem and Poser 1973; Ramp and Semb 1975; Kiernan and Woodford 1975).

The particular characteristics of mental handicap which the research of the time singled out as most significant, were an inability to learn incidentally or spontaneously as other children do, and non-transference of skills from one area of development to another (Clarke and Clarke 1974).

These difficulties are now viewed as the stock in trade of mental handicap and thus as defining characteristics of mentally handicapped children. They have a '...relative inability to profit from ordinary unstructured experience, a deficiency in spontaneous learning', which means that, 'It is virtually a defining characteristic of the subnormal child that he is unable to learn effectively - failure to learn is the basic psychological characteristic of subnormality' (Staff of Rectory Paddock School 1981, pp. 19 and 17).

Where attempts are made at the justification of suggested organisation, content and methodology, it is now commonplace to cite such learning difficulties of the mentally handicapped as a basis for the logical and moral necessity, and the efficacy, of highly structured and systematic programmes based on behavioural and skills analysis. For example:

> ... if we want to teach the child ... we have to... work out logically how the child might accomplish the task. ... We substitute systematic analysis and teaching for simple exposure, which may, with the handicapped child, lead to only very poor learning (C. Kiernan 1981 in the Forward).

Similarly, Gardner et al. discussing the need for a model in the education of severely mentally handicapped children and the demise of the nursery-/infant orientated programme of enrichment and experience, state that:

> Superficially, the argument for using nursery and infant methods of teaching seemed logical, on the basis that the children had low mental ages. But a 13 year old with a mental age of five years is not a 5 year old, and has very different needs, for example in terms of appropriate social skills training. Moreover, the methods employed in nursery and infant schools are inappropriate for severely mentally handicapped children who do not appear to learn incidentally from their environment, as do children who are not handicapped (Gardner et al. 1983 p. 13).

They go on to outline their 'Skills Analysis Model' as exemplary practice.

The scene depicted is one where 'research' has elucidated the learning difficulties and deficits of severely mentally handicapped children. An appropriate programme of remediation in the form of highly structured teaching has been outlined, which is claimed to overcome their difficulties and counteract deficits to the extent that this is possible given their permanent nature. This claim about the education of children with severe learning difficulties is now asserted in a very general manner, which takes the nature of mental handicap virtually for granted and therefore portrays educational needs in relation to mental handicap as self evident truths. This is somewhat in contrast to much of the research evidence about the learning difficulties of mentally handicapped children, originally used as the theoretical base of the objectives/skills analysis approach, which tended to concentrate on highly specific aspects of cognition in tightly controlled experimental situations. A leap has been made from this very specific research evidence to generalised claims for the necessity of a particular type of education and teaching. What is important to note is firstly that implicit in the calls for structured teaching is the idea that mentally handicapped childrens' characteristics require it. Its necessity, and by implication its efficacy, is therefore seen to have a solid base in scientific inquiry. Secondly, this further implies that structured teaching for mentally handicapped children is, by its very own nature, correct. It represents the answer and as such takes on the role of 'treatment' – the childrens' deficits are permanent but they can be made of less consequence by specific forms of education and training. There is no cure, but structured education can alleviate the 'symptoms' to some degree.

Curricula, as plans for instruction, along the lines of the objectives/skills analysis approach now exist, or are being produced in schools, as documents specifying aims, objectives, areas of development, organisation, methodology for assessment, teaching and evaluation.

Furthermore, moves towards a highly structured curriculum for children with severe learning difficulties, based on the objectives model and using skills analysis, have been officially endorsed as representing good practice by the Department of Education and Science (DES). Pamphlet 60 (DES 1975) proclaimed the universality of the broad aims of education, and emphasised the need for the curriculum for mentally handicapped children to be practically oriented and concerned with skills which were relevant to the pupils' needs with regard to developing independence. It also talked about the usefulness of highly structured programmes. The Warnock Report defined the aims of education for all children more precisely as:

> ... to enlarge a child's knowledge, experience and imaginative understanding, and thus his awareness of moral values and capacity for enjoyment; and... to enable him to enter the world after formal education is over, as an active participant in society and a responsible contributor to it, capable of achieving as much independence as possible (Warnock 1978 1:4).

The Warnock Report then proceeded to put forward the principle of determining educational needs in relation to the broad aims, thus defining special education in relation to the kind and amount of specialised help required to get a child some way along the path towards their attainment. Warnock also defined the curriculum in terms of the objectives model, in line with the idea that education should be geared towards specific ends generally thought desirable. It further noted the presence of 'well-defined' guidelines for each area of the curriculum, and 'programmes ... planned for individual children with clearly defined short term goals within the general plan' (Warnock 1978 11:5), as important criteria of high quality and effective special education.

Since the passing of the 1981 Education Act the structured approach based on the objectives model and skills analysis has been further endorsed as specifically suitable for the child with severe learning difficulties. In the first place the assessment procedure for statementing requires any child's strengths and weaknesses to be described in terms of such categories as cognitive functioning, communication skills, perceptual and motor skills, social skills and interaction (DES Circular 1/83). Secondly, it is suggested that the special educational provision required in response to the special educational needs of the child is specified in terms of aims of provision in general areas of development - physical, motor, cognitive, language and social (Ibid). The areas referred to here represent the categorical distinctions used in the objectives/skills analysis approach to the curriculum. Its usefulness is therefore emphatically endorsed with regard to delineating and remedying special educational needs, as well as the assessing of these needs, thus taking on the aims-objectives guise to educational planning and provision. Thirdly, the DES has actually proposed a definition of the curriculum felt suitable for the special educational needs of children with severe learning difficulties - this is 'developmental'.

> A curriculum covering selected and sharply focused educational, social and other experiences with precisely defined objectives and designed to encourage a measure of personal autonomy. Children needing such a curriculum may be described as having severe learning difficulties (DES 1984a p.2 para 3).

This categorically ratifies the new orthodoxy in the approach to the curriculum and educational programme planning for children with severe learning difficulties.

THE NEW ORTHODOXY
In terms of the curriculum for children with severe learning difficulties the new orthodoxy consists of the following major elements.

The Purpose of Education
The purpose of education as defined by broad, long term aims, is the same for all children, namely, personal development including awareness of moral values and development of the level of competence to participate in and contribute to life in society, achieving as much independence as possible. The aims are taken to refer to end products, that is, what might be achieved by the end of a course in education. The special educational needs of children with severe learning difficulties may dictate, 'WHAT they have to be taught and ... HOW ... but the point of their education is the same' (Warnock 1978 1:10). Its quality is to be seen in relation to 'the extent to which it leads a pupil towards the twin goals which we have described' (Warnock 1978 1:6). Personal autonomy, the concept used by Pamphlet 60 (DES 1975) and by the DES in their latest documentation

1975) and by the DES in their latest documentation
with reference to the aims of the developmental
curriculum, is conflated with 'independence' and
seen in a pragmatic way as what a person should be
able to do at the end of a course of compulsory
education. Autonomy, then, is seen as something
which comes along with independence and
independence hinges upon being competent in looking
after oneself, participating and contributing to
society in an acceptable manner, i.e. in a way
which conforms to norms of behaviour, convention
and law. Gunzberg describes this aptly:

> In the case of the mentally handicapped child,
> the primary educational goal should be modest
> but realistic: to assist in the maximum
> development of his social potential and to
> enable him to function later on in his
> particular adult community as unobtrusively
> and as competently as possible. This means
> that he must become socially acceptable and be
> able to contribute, if he can, to his own
> support, so that he is, at least, less
> dependent on his immediate environment
> (Gunzberg 1974b p. 628).

In the style of the 1980s, the purpose of
education for children with severe learning
difficulties tends to be translated either into
aims which emphasise as much independence as
possible and consequently the possibility of living
within the community, or aims which emphasise
becoming more normal. For example, Gardner et al.
suggest the general educational aim to be: 'To
teach the children in the school skills which will
be necessary for independent living in the
community' (Gardner et al. 1983 p.27). The Staff
of Rectory Paddock School suggest: 'The aim of
helping pupils to achieve more normal standards of
performance so far as possible' (Staff of Rectory
Paddock School 1981 p. 9), and Kiernan suggests,
'Objectives should bring the child as near to
normal behaviour as possible' (Kiernan 1981 p. 3).

The Delineation of 'Education'
What constitutes education is defined in areas
of development, e.g. cognitive, physical, motor,
self-help, social and leisure. Terms are
understood differently in different publications,
and in different schools, but such areas of
development, analogous to parts of the body's

functions and particular aspects of development from childhood to maturity, are specified as if they were subject headings. They form a conceptual framework in which to represent groups of skills and behaviours which relate to the aims of education and which come to constitute the content of the educational programme in a hierarchical, skill-building manner.

A typical example is the Copewell Curriculum (Whelan, Speake and Strickland 1984). This is divided into four main sectors - self-help, social academic, interpersonal and vocational. Each area is then broken down into various components. To take 'Interpersonal' as a case in hand, the Copewell curriculum suggests that skills in this area are covered by the headings - bodily awareness, personal knowledge, social interaction and social responsibility. Under each heading there appears a list of target behaviours which tend to be presented as if they represent both a developmental and hierarchical sequence; that is, as if particular targets have to be achieved before others can be achieved, and single or groups of targets have to be mastered before the young person can go on to do something else which has some kind of link with them. An example of this is demonstrated clearly in the component 'Bodily Awareness' -

16.1 Knowledge of body parts (male)
Can name and locate different parts of the male body.
16.2 Knowledge of body parts (female)
Can name and locate different parts of the female body.
16.3 Knowledge of body measurements and clothing sizes (male).
Can state his body measurements and related clothing sizes.
16.4 Knowledge of body measurements and clothing sizes (female).
Can state her body measurements and related clothing sizes.
16.5 Sexual Knowledge
Knows own sex and understands the basic differences between men and women and function of sexual organs.

(Whelan, Speake and Strickland 1984, p. 95).

Whether intentional or not, the presentation of targets in this manner is suggestive of a particular sequence for teaching and acquisition.

Furthermore, the placing of a particular set of targets before other areas of development and their targets (for instance, in this component area, before targets about social interaction including conduct in personal relationships, expressing and understanding feelings, recognising and showing responsibility in friendships) suggests that some targets are of a lower order than others. Their acquisition is therefore pre-requisite to the young people being able to meaningfully act at higher levels of competence, mastering higher order targets.

This kind of organisation and presentation of what is to be taught, and thus what is seen to represent education, is repeated with only slight variations throughout the literature, and throughout the development of curricula in schools catering for children with severe learning difficulties. The only diversion from this kind of typology appears specifically at the level of teaching mentally handicapped young people and adults, when education may be defined directly as skills the young people will require to function adequately in their particular present and future environments. However in this case, it is simply that the framework used is more to do with functionality than with academic classifications such as 'cognitive'. It may therefore refer to skills required in particular environments such as rooms within a house. For example, the skills needed in the bathroom might be identified as using the toilet, bathing, shaving, washing, cleaning teeth. The framework itself is still used to elucidate sets of skills and behaviours to be taught.

Teaching for the Child's Needs

Needs are identified by compiling a profile of what the child specifically can/can't do in relation to selected sequences of behavioural objectives within each curriculum area. What needs to be taught is shown up by the blank spaces on the recording sheet, wherever an objective hasn't been mastered and the appropriate box ticked. Assessment is therefore integral to choosing what to teach, and also in deciding whether or not teaching has been successful. The criterion is an increase in the desired behavioural repertoire, i.e. more ticks in more boxes. The Progress Assessment Chart (Gunzberg 1966) and the Portage Guide to Early Education (Shearer and Shearer 1972)

paved the way with the specification of targets
under developmental headings, ranging from low
level simple skills to higher level complex skills
in a chronological manner. The Behaviour Assessment Battery (Kiernan and Jones 1977), The British
Institute of Mental Handicap's Developmental Checklists (Perkins et al. 1976), The Path Project
(Jeffree and Cheseldine 1982) and most recently
'The Skills Analysis Model' (Gardner et al. 1983)
and the Copewell Curriculum (Whelan, Speake and
Strickland 1984) have extended this approach, as
have many 'core' curricula in individual special schools. Other developmental areas have been
delineated and broken down into their different skill sets and teaching targets, supposedly producing a comprehensive compendium of
everything the child needs to learn to be able to
act as independently as possible.

In terms of assessment the emphasis is upon
criterion referenced targets where the conditions
and the number of times a task has to be achieved
are specified so as to objectify success and ensure
that the child's performance is only being judged
in reference to his own previous performance. This
is significantly different from standardised tests
such as traditional IQ tests and checklists of
normal developmental milestones, formally used as
the mainstay of assessment, which compared the
child's performance to the norm in a simplistic
manner, very often giving global scores and no
direction as to what it was appropriate to teach.
The child is ostensibly only competing against
himself. Nonetheless, target behaviours are drawn
from norm referenced skill sets and are those which
it is thought children with severe learning difficulties need to acquire, rather than indicators of
particular levels of development. Gardner et al
make the point that core areas (and by implication
their components and targets) should be concerned
with skill development, rather than general experiences, and with 'vital areas of mastery learning for all children; necessary elements of learning which lead to the attainment of the school's
educational aim' (Gardner et al. 1983, p. 27). Assessment, and by implication teaching, since one
informs the other, are therefore directly related
to the indentification and fulfillment of what are
seen as the child's needs, because needs are defined in terms of a lack of a mastery of vital
skills, and education is about teaching for
mastery of these self-same skills.

A Task and Skill Oriented Curriculum

It follows that education in the special school is about teaching the child to perform certain tasks rather than giving him broad educational experiences. The required end products of teaching for children with severe learning difficulties are specified beforehand. The stated aims of education are translated into sets of target behaviours describing 'what the child is expected to do in order for the teacher to say that a component such as the feeding or toileting component of the self-help core area has been learned' (Gardner et al. 1983, p. 29). Targets are written for each seperate skill which makes up a component broken down into steps for teaching by skills and then task analysis. The steps represent tasks which the child must achieve if he is to reach criterion performance of the target behaviour.

Not all the published literature on curriculum development for children with severe learning difficulties goes as far as presenting the breakdown of targets by task analysis into teachable units, ostensibly because individual children can cope with different size steps from one task to another and many task analyses may be produced to teach the same target to different children. However, it is clear that task analysis, either explicitly or implicitly, represents the method of translating targets as objectives to be achieved, into a teaching programme. What follows is that teaching and education is concerned with getting the child to be able to complete specific tasks correctly.

Teaching Life Skills

As indicated earlier, the emphasis is on teaching for needs which are determined in relation to the mastery of necessary skills. The importance of the chosen skills is claimed to lie in their usefulness for independent living. Although to be as independent as possible is seen as part of the universal aims of education and therefore applicable to all children the emphasis placed directly on teaching specific skills which are seen as necessary for independent living is exceptional in the education of children with severe learning difficulties. Nowhere else in the education sector is there the same emphasis on teaching such things as self-help skills like feeding, dressing, toileting, through to the use of public transport, survival cookery and basic shopping skills, or such an intense effort to develop communication skills, however basic. Nor is there such a direct attempt at teaching socially acceptable behaviour, like not swearing or spitting on the bus. Such 'skills' are not usually directly taught - at least not by teachers in school. They are among the great many skills that ordinary children pick up 'incidentally' in the course of everyday life, and which, it is firmly believed, children with severe learning difficulties miss out on because of their incidental learning deficit, and their difficulty in generalising and adapting learning to new situations. Hence their need to be taught such skills and the justification and motivation for education to consist, in the main, of ordinary, everyday knowledge which is not usually taught to children in the formal sense of the word. This is what the DES (1984a and c) now refer to as the 'developmental' curriculum - the overall purpose of education may be universal, but the content and method of teaching differ markedly from that employed in other spheres of education.

The assumption underlying this formulation of education is that components and targets making up the curriculum are vital for any individual to be independent. ALL the targets are therefore necessary. Individuals only differ in how many skills they have already acquired or are likely to gain. Mental handicap is seen in relation to 'normality' and is defined in terms of social competence and acceptance, or lack of potential for these, because of the presence of the condition of mental handicap.

Individualisation

It follows from what has already been said about the curriculum that the other major element is individualisation. Objectives are for the individual, specified in relation to the assessment of his needs. Needs are defined in terms of the next steps along the developmental ladder from the individual's present performance towards his acquisition of skills for 'life', until in the adolescent years objectives may be tightly defined in terms of the individual's prospective future. Targets are broken down into incremental steps to suit the learning capacity of the individual child - an individual programme for individualised objectives. The result is an educational programme which is geared to the individual's requirements in terms of the overall aims of education, recognising the heterogeneity of the 'mentally handicapped' population; their different ability levels and hence their individual needs.

Several points arise out of the curriculum for children with severe learning difficulties as it is put forward by the specialists in the field, and as is being expressed in the curricula being developed in the country's special schools, which are not made explicit in the literature concerning the skills analysis approach. We would specifically like to draw attention to the following.

Firstly, skills usually learned informally are formalised by the skills analysis approach to the curriculum. In claiming that there are specific sets of skills in developmental areas, the acquisition of which leads to a more normal appearance and an ability to live independently in the community, it is being assumed that such skills represent entrance qualifications to mainstream life and culture. The status of these skills for mentally handicapped people is thus raised in relation to their status for the ordinary population. By definition, the mentally handicapped person is unable to attain these skills, in the first place, in an ordinary manner, and without them he will remain mentally handicapped. Hence the need for special education and the developmental curriculum as described by the DES.

Secondly, the criteria of success implied by the formalisation of ordinary skills becomes, for the child with severe learning difficulties, the acquisition of skills. Success becomes defined in terms of getting ticks on to the record sheets where before there were blank spaces.

Thirdly, the present objectives/skills analysis approach implies that a specific teaching methodology is best and most efficient because it establishes the required learning in the child, leaving little, if any room for error. This methodology begins with the delineation of behavioural objectives for individual pupil outcomes and then employs what were called in the mid-1970s, behaviour modification techniques - i.e. task analysis, One-to-One teaching situations, the application of rewards, negative reinforcement and punishment, through prompting, shaping and chaining, and the development of criterion referenced assessment (Vargas 1977; Poteet 1973; Axelrod 1977; Wedell 1975; Kiernan and Woodford 1975). The basic ideas behind such techniques used to be known simply as good teaching practice, but were extended and put across in a much more rigorous and precise form within the behavioural mode (e.g. Education of the Developmentally Young project - EDY). The fact that such techniques were connected with behaviour modification and behaviourism is now, however, not always acknowledged. Kiernan et al. suggest that 'the methods are basic to nearly all learning' (Kiernan et al. 1978, p. 23), and in other places they are referred to as 'precision-teaching' methods (Raybould and Solity 1982). The elucidation of these techniques so that they are now commonly available for teaching practice, arms the teacher with systematic means of assessment, teaching and evaluation of learning as well as task analysis sheets, trial sheets, and checklists to record progress and show precisely what she has been teaching, and what the pupil has mastered. The popularity of EDY (Education of the Developmentally Young Project, 1978) and SNAP (Special Needs Action Programme, 1983), both of which are inservice training courses for teachers of children with special educational needs, and which include teaching packages about methodology along the lines sketched out above, bear witness to the enthusiasm with which this specific teaching methodology has been greeted as a successful means of educating traditionally difficult and/or different children.

Fourthly, the curriculum, and thus education, is seen primarily in terms of performance rather than experiencing or even understanding. It is about knowing (not necessarily understanding) certain identifiable bodies of knowledge (body parts, how to get on the bus or how to cross the road) which inform behaviour in different settings. At the same time it is also concerned with changing children: 'The only way we can hope to change children, and know we have succeeded, is to change their behaviour. This is the basis for the use of an objectives approach to the curriculum' (Leeming et al. 1979, p. 68).

This is not to suggest that the whole educational programme for children with severe learning difficulties is now a matter of One-to-One teaching of tasks, the teacher being armed with her task analysis and core curriculum sheets. Rather, practice in schools tends to oscillate between structured teaching sessions where children are

working on individual programmes incorporating
individualised objectives and possibly One-to-One
teaching, and much less structured and less
individualised activities such as visits out in the
mini-bus, 'free' time when the children may choose
different activities, and other types of group
activities such as singing, dancing or horse
riding. Sometimes the idea of individualised
objectives may permeate all activities offered so
that a teacher may have particular things in mind
for different children when they are swimming or
dancing, visiting a cafe or museum. However, there
tends to be a clear distinction between what
represents a time for direct teaching, and what
represents opportunities for skills learned to be
generalised and transferred to other less formal
situations.

At the theoretical level, the need for a
'balanced' curriculum is referred to, and the
concepts of open/closed curriculum, and
mastery/awareness of bodies of knowledge have been
invoked. These have provided both a framework for
curriculum development and a description of what
was actually happening, or of what people felt
should happen. Simultaneously they guard against
the view of education for children with severe
learning difficulties being not dissimilar to
child-minding, and the danger of thrusting too much
at teachers and pupils in terms of the imperative
to achieve. The concepts of open/closed and
mastery/awareness in curriculum development
conceptualised balance between structured teaching
and enrichment activities, thus providing a
framework in which both can be seen as important.
It also allows space for those who argue that it is
impossible to teach on a One-to-One basis for much
of the time because of the constraints upon
classroom teachers, or to adhere to a tight
syllabus because of the nature of the children's
learning difficulties (their deficits and the
unpredictability of their development).

However, it is also clear that the distinction
between open/closed, mastery/awareness or
structured teaching/enrichment activities, has come
to represent a distinction between what is and what
isn't education, or at least what lies on the
periphery of education, and that this further
relates to a distinction between work and play, or
fun.

The closed curriculum represents core units of
knowledge to be built up by the mastery of

objectives crucial to developing independence. The open curriculum allows for the provision of experiences which will provide the child with an awareness of other areas of knowledge which can balance the highly systematic teaching required by the closed curriculum. The emphasis within education for children with severe learning difficulties lies firmly with the closed curriculum and mastery of skills. The development of the whole idea of the core curriculum illustrates this process as it occured during the 1970s to date, as educationalists searched for a framework for the education of these children as distinct from their training or occupation, and thus a definition, subsequently of what the content of their education should be. The development of the core curriculum was essentially about the closed curriculum and about outlining those skills which had to be mastered, rather than experiences which it might be beneficial to present. Kiernan describes the present situation succinctly when he suggests that - '... the behavioural approach (which is aligned to the closed curriculum) is less easily identified as a 'fun' approach and more easily identified as 'education' by parents and teachers alike' (Kiernan 1980, p. 23: our insertion).

Kiernan's comment also points to a further development in the movement towards structured teaching and the use of the objectives/skills analysis approach. Even though there may still be considerable variation as to what actually happens in individual schools, there is considerable pressure to adopt the particular curriculum style and content of objective/skills analysis described above, as it refers to the closed curriculum and mastery of skills, rather than enrichment activities. Whereas in 1974 Cunningham noted that:

Unfortunately we do not possess ... organised knowledge of content (subject matter and instructional methods) ... the present picture is one of confusion. In particular teachers do not appear to have a reference framework against which to set standards and assess progress, to interrelate activities within and between classrooms and beyond the school to later life (Cunningham 1974, p. 48: our insertion).

Now it is claimed there is such a 'reference frame

work and organised knowledge of content'. For example Gardner et al. suggest that they are offering, for severely mentally handicapped children:

> ... a curriculum which has clear objectives in terms of specified skills (which) will permit careful assessment of each child's abilities and will enable selection of an appropriate item as the next teaching target for that individual. It will provide a structure by means of which the student is enabled to proceed, by small steps through a hierarchy of skills, which is not based on normative developmental data, but on the breakdown of target skills into constituent elements by a process of skills or task analysis (Gardner et al. 1983, p. 20).

Indeed, their Skills Analysis Model does do all this, and as such, epitomises the new orthodoxy in curriculum development for children with severe learning difficulties.

Pressure to adopt the objectives/skills analysis approach has, however, not simply arisen from its forceful presentation as <u>the</u> answer by those in the position of recognised and acknowledged authority in the field of the education of mentally handicapped children, although it has definitely enjoyed a somewhat monopolistic position. There are other reasons relating to various movements in the education system and wider society, and to specific historical circumstances which have meant that curriculum development along the skills analysis paradigm was a logical development and almost inevitable given the dominant perception of mental handicap as unable and education as instrumental. However it is sufficient to note here, that the DES's definition of the 'developmental' curriculum is one that implies that this curriculum model already occurs and is an acceptable, meaningful and effective way of 'educating' children with severe learning difficulties.

Schools are now being required to define and present their curricula according to: the 1980 Education Act (which requires certain details about the school to be made public); the assessment procedure of the 1981 Education Act (Circular 1/83 and Education Regulations 1983); Circular 6/81 [which made it clear that all schools will be required to have a written statement of their aims and the

content of their curriculum]; and A Note by the DES
'The Organisation and content of the Curriculum:
Special Schools' October 1984.   This means that: -
1) not only has the objectives/skills analysis
approach been officially defined as meeting the
special educational needs of children with severe
learning difficulties, but also;
2)   teachers and schools are being constrained to
think about, and present, their curriculum in particular ways which, in the case of schools catering
for children with severe learning difficulties, are
not only congruent with the objectives/skills analysis approach, but actually embody it as a definition of what constitutes 'education' for these
children.

Chapter Two

LEARNING TO BE INDEPENDENT?

The conceptualisation of the educational programme
in terms of core curriculum areas consisting of
specific skills to be learned has provided answers
to the question of WHAT to teach children with
severe learning difficulties. The suggested methodology for programme planning and teaching itself,
has provided answers to the question of HOW to
teach them. The aims of education and the special
educational needs of children with severe learning
difficulties provide answers to the questions of
what it is all for, and why this content this
methodology. The teacher is provided with a
specific framework which not only gives her
direction, but also offers her specific means of
justifying and legitimating her practice. At the
same time her accountability to others has been
increased - at least in terms of producing the
paper work.

HANDICAPPING CONDITIONS: THE IMPLICATIONS OF THE
NEW ORTHODOXY
     For children with severe learning difficulties
the consequences of the objectives/skills analysis
approach are, however, simply to confirm the
children's dependence, their inabilities and
difference from the norm. It confirms that they
are devalued people, mentally handicapped children
- that is, that their most significant attribute is
their mental handicap, it pervades everything they
do, and is their problem since it is a condition
inside them (in their brains). The
objectives/skills analysis approach presents a view
of education and the task of educating, which does
not challenge the objectification and dehumanisation of mentally handicapped people. Instead,
objectification and dehumanisation are enshrined in

the pseudo-scientific apparatus of the individualised curriculum for children with severe learning
difficulties who will doubtless become mentally
handicapped adults. Limitation of opportunities and
rights are legitimated by recourse to a concept of
specific needs which disallows the mentally handicapped child's responsibility for his own actions.
The reproduction of stereotypes attached to
negative values, and to fear and pity for those who
are seen to be less than fully human, is reinforced. Such consequences differ significantly
from the intended outcomes specifically stated as
aims and objectives of the curriculum. They may be
unintentional, in the sense that they are not
planned and in the sense that they are not
recognised as consequences by the establishment in
general which continues to adhere to the ideology
of the rehabilitative nature of special educational
provision.

For children with severe learning
difficulties, these predominantly unrecognised
consequences of the curriculum converge to help
create and maintain handicapping conditions within
the special education system and within other
social situations on which it bears. This happens
because -
1) the particular characteristics of the ob-
jectives/skills analysis approach have serious
implications with regard to the social construction
of handicap, as a disadvantage and a negative
status conferred on people with impairments by
other people, and by the structure of the social
and educational systems in which all people exist.
2) at the same time there is no recognition of the
differentiation of impairment, disability and
handicap within the orthodox view of the special
educational needs of children with severe learning
difficulties and the special educational provision
they are therefore seen to require. Consequently,
within special education for children with severe
learning difficulties, no notion exists of how
handicap can be a result of well intentioned
people's actions, and the organisation of a system
which is itself viewed as offering something
intrinsically good and beneficial to any individual
- that is, education.

The Promotion of a Means - Ends Curriculum

The objectives/skills analysis approach
promotes a means - ends curriculum, rather than a
process oriented curriculum. Education is viewed

as a vehicle to future situations. The great danger of concentrating on end products is that, '... we impose our understanding on children without giving them a chance to develop their own understanding. That is not education' (McConkey 1981, p. 9). Inherent in this view of education is therefore the possibility of imposing arbitrary limitations on what is taught and learned. The pre-occupation with end products - making children with severe learning difficulties more normal, better behaved, more acceptable - means that 'success', or the prognosis for its possibility, is measured against the concept of the end product, normality. The degree of a child's handicap is defined by the number of ticks he has achieved on the evaluation sheets, the progress record sheet or some other measuring device. However complex their filling-in is and whatever new name they are called by, they still represent the old idea of the check-list and this can now be regarded as on a parallel with the examination system in ordinary schools.

The Restricted View of Work and its Implicit Place in the Aims of Education

By aiming at independence, the concept of work, of being able to support oneself, or at least contribute to upkeep, is implicit as one of the ultimate goals of education. However, 'work' tends to be narrowly defined as meaning productive, paid labour of a traditional kind, since the labour market and its requirements for workers to fit in are taken as given. The objectives relating to preparation for adulthood therefore include skills which allow for fitting in - competence in self-help skills, and no bizarre behaviour. The co-operative model of work, or capitalising on particular skills and interests students have as a means of 'work' are not commonly seen as alternatives (Beresford et al. 1982).

The Restricted View of Normality

The conception of education as a means to an end, and the upholding of traditional open employment as one of the significant criteria of success within the educational enterprise, are based on a correspondingly narrow view of normality - as an ideal type to aim for. The assumption is that a mentally handicapped person will only be able to live and participate within the community if he displays certain skills, attitudes and behaviours. 'The teachers said that ATCs did not welcome some students; the same ones we would expect the labour market to reject; those clearly needing support "with little language, disruptive", not toilet trained, disturbed, who can't fit in' (Beresford et al. 1982, p. 237).

Furthermore, standards of behaviour are imposed on children with severe learning difficulties which may not be upheld by many ordinary people who are not labelled mentally handicapped, such as tidiness, being well groomed, and neatly dressed, saying please and thank you. This is recognised by many teachers and other professionals when they remark that mentally handicapped people must behave better than ordinary children and adults in order to be accepted in social situations and community settings.

The Use of Normative Assessment

Assessment for teaching is normative, i.e. finding out the deficiencies in comparison with the sets of skills assumed to be necessary for development to the independent life maintained by ordinary people.

The Prominence of Individualism

Assessment is furthermore exclusively individualised, expressing practically the ideology of the special needs of individual pupils. Since within the objectives/skills analysis model assessment is directly linked to what and how to teach, teaching in the closed curriculum is also almost exclusively individualised - individual programmes working towards individual objectives, and for the most part seen to demand individualised teaching.

The Power Given to Teachers and Schools

The teacher and the school are in the position of -
1) defining what is important and necessary in order to be able to live in the community and;
2) defining the child's needs in relation to this axis, i.e. deciding the child's future requirements.

The Emphasis on Performance

The objectives/skills analysis approach emphasises doing, which may be at the sake of understanding. It teaches efficient performances, but these do not necessarily represent thinking performances, or create means of applying learning

29

to new situations and developing the strategies
for coping and participating in them. The emphasis
is on the individual completing the task, rather
than the processes involved and their application
for generalisation and spontaneous use of skills.
The objectives/skills analysis approach to teaching
children with severe learning difficulties has not
generally come in for much criticism, but the
little that has been expressed in England, has
mainly stemmed from this particular concern.
McConkey (1981) and B. Smith et al. (1983) have
pointed to the limitations of the objectives/skills
analysis approach in this regard. They have also
backed up their articles with research evidence
which suggests that direct One-to-One teaching, in
highly structured situations, may not be the
panacea it is held up to be if understanding and
progressive development are priorities rather than
just performance.

The above have concrete effects. They mean
that to start with, children are seen in terms of
deficits, what they can't do. The objectives/
skills analysis approach is reductionist in that
its emphasis is on teaching discrete skills upon
which other areas of adaptive functioning are seen
to hinge. Teachers are being directed to teach
children the logical intervention targets of a
reductionist approach - those skills lacking in the
crucial repertoire of things they can do.
The emphasis upon defining and remediating
deficits in functioning, in comparison to the
yardstick of crucial skills, highlights
abnormalities and difference from the 'norm'. The
assumption that such deficits are in need of
remediation devalues, if not ignores, any positive
contribution the child with severe learning
difficulties might make and what he has to offer to
the rest of us as a person in his own right.
The constant individualisation within the
educational programme brings with it the dominant
value structure which upholds the primacy of
individual effort and responsibility at the expense
of group collaboration and group responsibility,
blaming the individual for his own failure: 'Those
who fail must blame themselves (for lack of
persistence, ability or the vicissitudes of fate)'
(Shapiro 1980, p. 222). The responsibility for
deficits is left with the child, such deficits and
inabilities being expressions or symptoms of his
'mental handicap'. Although environmental factors

may be manipulated within the prominent behavioural teaching methodology, which does not, at the teaching level, impute failure to 'mental handicap', the objectives/skills analysis approach is still saying that: 'What he really needs is to be normal, and we can't make him normal, its a question of cognitive ability' (Serpell-Morris 1982, p. 179).

The objectives/skills analysis approach as a means-ends curriculum, continues to define 'needs' in reference to circumstances external to the child which present pressures to acquire and master certain skills, attitudes and behaviours in order for other opportunities and other life circumstances to be granted and made available. It is based on an imperative of future participation in communities which are at present closed to the mentally handicapped person. This is assumed to be because of the child's inabilities and unusual behaviour which make him unacceptable as an equal member of the community.

The present approach is about teaching discrete skills. Frequently they are functional skills in the sense that such skills are useful to individuals in terms of being independent in a very practical way - e.g. how to dress, eat, use the toilet, get about, wash, cross the road, go shopping, use money, ask for what you want in the cafe. Knowledge is not taught in an abstract and 'academic' way (at least not in most schools catering for children with severe learning difficulties), where the child is expected to transfer and generalise his knowledge to the skills needed in everyday life. But teaching discrete, albeit functional skills, is about creating normal appearances. It is not about learning to be independent except in the narrowest of definitions. For children with severe learning difficulties and mentally handicapped people, independence remains elusive.

For example, children who eat with a knife and fork and sit quietly at the table, look more normal and are less conspicuous than those who eat with their fingers, or throw the plate across the floor. Discrete, functional skills provide a 'cloak of competence' - '... the signs of normality which the retarded are required to produce before they are considered able to live in anything but a totally protective environment' (Bercovici 1983, p. 169). But a collection of practical skills doesn't make up an independent, participating and contributing member of the community. It doesn't necessarily follow that even the person with a wide repertoire of practical skills will be able to make decisions for himself - especially not those decisions which others consider to be about important issues, such as future placement, leaving home, taking medication, choosing friends and places to go; or that he will be able to develop and maintain relationships with others, or accept responsibility for his own actions and how these may impinge on others. The normal appearances and 'cloak of competence' afforded by being able to perform certain commonplace activities without aid, and not to give oneself away by bizarre behaviour, act as cosmetic devices.

Bercovici points out how in the case of physical disability, pressure is on, for example, eyeless or limbless people to wear prosthetic devices. She goes on to explain that,

> ...... members of a culture operate according to, and depend upon, certain cultural templates that define the real world. It is ordinarily disturbing and a cause for remedial action of one kind or another when objects, events and persons deviate from the prescriptions of the cultural world view. One kind of cultural effort to reduce the dissonance between real and ideal conditions are called normalisation ... The cultural definition of what is a human being includes an inventory of its constituent parts. An incomplete body is a source of discomfort and can even give rise to doubts on the parts of other cultural members whether, or to what extent, this being qualifies as human. So attempts may be made to normalise this form, even if only cosmetically (Bercovici 1983, p. 173).

Similarly, mentally handicapped people and children with severe learning difficulties display dissonance with an inventory of sets of skills ordinary people learn incidentally and tasks they can perform without any hint of difficulty. Teaching discrete, albeit functional skills is in this sense 'normalising' children with severe learning difficulties. As the Staff of Rectory Paddock School (1981) and Kiernan (1981) suggest, it is helping them achieve more normal standards of performance. But the activities have a cosmetic value in terms of the notion of independence, if value in terms of the notion of independence, if this is seen to include notions of self-determination and autonomy, within a social, that is an interactional community setting, and not just a freedom from physical manipulation because of the help otherwise needed to perform everyday bodily functions.

Within the dominant concept of education for children with severe learning difficulties, independence is confused with socialisation and socialisation has been conflated with the 'needs' of these children. As Chavert says in an uncritical vein about the curriculum for children with severe learning difficulties:

> It is based on the idea of educational socialisation. This attempts to fit a child into the background in which he is to live; to teach him the language, the correct behaviour, the habits and customs of the people around him. He learns to use the facilities of that civilisation and is taught the simple academic skills he will need. Such a teaching programme differs only in range, depth and timing from what is offered to young normal children. For the mentally handicapped child, it will cover his years at school and stretch into his further education. This then is the modified part of the curriculum as described by Warnock (Chavert 1979, p. 98).

The teacher is inevitably put in a position of making value judgements about the child's needs and what he should learn. It is the teacher who must decide which skills, of all skills are crucial, and which are relevant to the child's likely future, as well as his immediate 'need' to function adequately and acceptably within his present environment. The decisions made inherently reflect the teacher's viewpoint, her definition of what is important, and what is acceptable or unacceptable behaviour, referenced against skills which have already academically been valued as important for independence and community living by inclusion in published curricula, or the curriculum statement of the school. Serpell-Morris remarks:

> The inspectorate and the government are very keen on teacher accountability. And teacher accountability leads to curricula based on and around specific behavioural objectives. I see

33

this as a dangerous trend. If enough people are sufficiently entranced by it, it could reduce the possibility of teachers viewing handicapped people as human beings with a mind and lifestyle of their own and a need to be themselves. It leads to adults making these vulnerable people dance to their tune. They'll say "you will do this because I say you need to learn it". In other words it leads to people defining future needs for those who cannot respond (Serpell-Morris 1982, p. 178).

Although we would contend Serpell-Morris' last sentiment about mentally handicapped people's inability to respond, we would go further than him, suggesting that the state of affairs he fears, already exists. This is so in terms of what the government is sanctioning as good practice and the type of curriculum being urged upon teachers by authorities and researchers in the field. In addition there are the pressures presented by everyday existence in class, to cope and answer the questions of what and how to teach on a daily basis. As Serpell-Morris goes on to point out, what teachers may decide are children's 'needs' may, in fact, have nothing to do with their 'needs', their desires or wants, but may, instead, reflect the need to make life easier for those around the children, and the imperative to fit into what is given. As he puts it: '... the needs we identify have more to do with what society wants these children to be, than with what these children are' (Serpell-Morris 1982, p. 179). This attitude further highlights the devaluation of what children with severe learning difficulties can do, by reference to their presumed need to rectify what they can't do, and its relation to their status as human beings.

Furthermore, the position of the teacher, in defining the child's needs in relation to future requirements, explicitly places the pupil in a passive position where he has no real contribution to make to his own education. Rather, the child with severe learning difficulties is a recipient of education. Within the curriculum, the objectives and the teacher are the controlling factors. Important decisions regarding the pupil's everyday life conditions lie within the framework they offer, not within the pupil's frame of reference. Control of one sort or another over the pupil (e.g.

teacher control or the control of social conventions) is a major concern. Many objectives within the skills analysis approach are frequently expressed in terms of the pupil responding to external control measures. For example, the establishment of attention to the teacher and to set tasks, on the part of the pupil, in addition to the establishment of sitting down behaviour in order to perform set tasks. In this way the child's participation in his education as a person with rights to make decisions for himself, is not allowed for. He is provided with education. Behavioural methods have replaced rote learning and drill, but the difference seems more subtle than radical. The reference within the objectives/skills analysis approach to the provision of highly structured learning environments and 'precision teaching', via the use of the techniques of operant conditioning, seems somewhat euphemistic in our view.

As Shapiro says of the behaviouristic view of education - that based on behavioural objectives and skills analysis:

> ... it is an authoritarian approach to the process of education. Education becomes a process in which the student attempts to come as close as possible to the outcomes already anticipated by a teacher. It replaces a process that is open-ended and exploratory, with one that awards conformity with "correct" answers (Shapiro 1980, p. 221).

The content of the educational programme as the formalisation of skills and knowledge ordinarily learned in naturally occuring situations, itself becomes handicapping within the objectives/skills analysis approach. In raising the status of ordinary knowledge and skills to that of 'education' for children with severe learning difficulties, they take on an importance which is in extreme contrast to their significance for ordinary people. The emphasis placed on the child or young person with severe learning difficulties gaining such knowledge and skills misconstrues the relations of these competencies to ordinary states of life. It makes them have relations to opportunities and possibilities that they are not normally related to for the ordinary population. Bercovici gives many examples which illustrate this point well. One such example, taken from adult education is:

> Researcher - what do you have to do to get married?
> Marie - cook, sew, read, count money, tell time, add, subtract, stuff like that ...
> (Bercovici 1983, p. 170).

Marie's response clearly denotes the successful inculcation of the message of the objectives/skills analysis approach - that skills have to be mastered before independence/community living can be achieved. At the level of adulthood when ordinarily independence is granted, come what may, the fallacy is brought home.

It is not only that others are directly imposing limitations through the fallacious argument that particular skills have to be mastered in the artificial environment of the classroom before certain activities which the skills may or may not be related to can be indulged in outside of the classroom environment. As the example above shows, mentally handicapped people may themselves take on these definitions of abilities or inabilities, so handicapping themselves in the way of a self-fulfilling prophecy. The unfounded and unchallenged importance placed on the acquisition of basic skills can therefore effectively limit the mentally handicapped person's opportunities to participate and contribute to social situations, to develop relationships and to practise independence.

At the level of maturation and development there are obviously some things which a child has to be able to do before he can do other things - walk before he runs, hold a pencil before he can write. But these things tend to be about the development or limitations of our bodies, or our lack of knowledge either through direct or indirect experience of things. We should all be aware, for example, that because a child cannot talk, it does not mean that he cannot understand; lack of motor control does not mean a person cannot communicate; gross physical abnormalities do not mean that people do not have the same feelings as people who have none, and are any less capable of maintaining deep relationships, and living on their own or as couples.

At another level, many people may find it difficult to cope in public with a child whose behaviour may impinge on other people because the behaviour crosses the fine dividing line between behaviour crosses the fine dividing line between social acceptability and unacceptability. The responses of other people may make it difficult or embarassing to take a child on a public bus, if he spends most of his time screaming. Taking a child into a supermarket, if he is forever picking up things, especially edibles, may present difficulties. But this does not mean, necessarily, that the child should not be taken into these environments before he can consistently conform to the norms of behaviour related to them.

However, this is the kind of thinking which is embodied by the present view of education for children with severe learning difficulties as a means to specific ends, and is reinforced by the objectives/skills analysis approach. Skills are conceptualised, organised and presented in a hierarchical manner, to be mastered by the child completing specific targets. As McConkey has pointed out, the reasoning behind the present approach and probably one of the reasons for its popularity is that, ' ... the assumption we make is that the child's mastery of these highly specific tasks ... in some way is building up the child's repertoire of basic skills' (McConkey 1981, p. 9).

Inherent in the dominant view of education for children with severe learning difficulties is the idea that being able to do certain tasks - from putting pegs in holes, to tying shoelaces, to recognising the names of members of the class - is relevant and useful, not simply for its own sake but also because it leads to independence. The high status afforded to ordinary everyday knowledge in the education of these children has created the fallacy of the 'when-then' approach: i.e. when he has mastered ring stacking then he can go on to the peg board; when he can recognise the number of the bus, sit quietly on the bus, and get off at the right stop, then he can go on the bus to college, as long as he is supervised. As the example about 'what you have to do to get married' begins to show, this kind of thinking relates to false defin- itions of abilities and inabilities, as well as a total failure to recognise the ways in which handi- cap is socially defined and constructed. Mastery of particular tasks is taken to indicate a certain level of ability, whereas incompetence at particu- lar tasks relates to a conception of inability, and in both cases ability or inability is perceived by those around the child, in global terms, rather than in relation to specific tasks.

Learning to be Independent?

Furthermore, it appears that as well as assuming that particular skills add up to basic independent living skills, it is also being assumed that those strategies which are not directly taught within the objectives/skills analysis approach, but which are part of a common sense definition of independence - self regulation, self control, decision making, interactional skills, group membership, consequences and their relation to responsibilities - are acquired indirectly. It is being assumed that strategies for determining one's own lifestyle within a community, rather than merely functioning adequately within it, come 'naturally' once a person has reached a certain (unspecified) level of skills in looking after himself practically and a certain level of inter-action with the community (determined by the level of skill). This assumption is parallelled by a belief that before a person has certain skills or capabilities associated with a developing practical independence, that person is incapable of making decisions for himself in a meaningful fashion. He is unable, therefore, to know what is in his best interests.

In the light of the assumptions about their particular learning difficulties, it seems somewhat contradictory then to assume that children with severe learning difficulties will either pick up what decision making strategies, self control, self- determination and interactional strategies they are capable of, alongside the teaching of specific skills; or that as young people they will acquire such strategies in their daily lives, if they are so capable. However, this paradox is assuaged by the presentation of both the curriculum process and the content to be taught as logical sequences which are both chronological and hier-archical in nature. Thus the supposed derivation of objectives from aims, and the belief that their achievement leads towards aims, suggests that the ends themselves are idealised end states. This gives justification to the argument that certain skills have to be mastered before other skills and strategies can be acquired. Decision making, self control, self determination, are presumed to be 'skills' at the pinnacle of 'independence' and thus the practical expression of the aims of education. In this sense such skills seem to be understood as strategies which may be acquired later, after an educational lifetime, for which education lays the groundwork. The adherence to the doctrine of aims

38

as idealistic and therefore probably unobtainable (e. g. Cunningham 1974), further justifies the lack of emphasis placed on these strategies to the extent that mentally handicapped people are by-definition seen to be incapable of such notions of independence.

Initially, the educational experience of children with severe learning difficulties is abnormal, in terms of attending a separate, usually small and not local school which they are bussed or taxied to, often for the whole of their school lives. Inevitably, within the present dominant value system which celebrates competition and material success, stigma is attached to special education with its association to low status i.e. non-academic knowledge and the pupil failures of the education system. Within special education, children with severe learning difficulties are identified as part of the 'mentally handicapped', as if they represented an homogenous group. Although the 1981 Education Act seems to get away from the direct relationship between handicap and types of education felt suitable, the Statement procedure gives a new guise for the old practices by asking for the curriculum aims and methodology within a normative framework. The assumption that children with severe learning difficulties need a highly structured and specific curriculum leads many children to the old ESN(S) schools, simply by a more complicated route, parading as the identification of individual 'needs' and the provision of individual programmes to fulfil those 'needs'.

The design and implementation of the dominant objectives/skills analysis approach extends the abnormal educational, socialisation conditions. It utilises a content and methodology which emphasises the failures of these children, in comparison with their 'normal' peers, in the things to which educational success generally is seen to lead to - status, money, work and identification as a legitimate participant and contributor in the community.

Independence, in its fullest sense, mainly follows from employment in our society, where the work ethic is still dominant. But, ' ... the labour market largely and increasingly excludes such young people (severely mentally handicapped people) from work, except in its most marginal, menial, insecure and poorly paid sectors' (Beresford et al. 1982, p. 242). Pupils instead progress to ATCs (Adult Training Centres) when there is a place. Residential communities are the only other major alternative. As Beresford et al. note, schools catering for children with severe learning difficulties, ' ... serve as a dumping ground for the rejects of mainstream schooling, who in turn become the rejects of the labour market' (Ibid., p. 242).

Children with severe learning difficulties, as mentally handicapped people, ostensibly cannot get jobs because they cannot do the job, or others can do it better because they are not mentally handicapped. Without work mentally handicapped people cannot, at the very least, be financially independent (e.g. Wertheimer 1981). They are caught up in a vicious circle which revolves around opportunities for living, education and work.

Mentally handicapped people are defined as dependents in the first place, on account of their disabilities. They are taught particular skills of physical independence by the present curriculum, but 'independence' in its broader sense is not allowed for because of: -

1) the narrow concept of mental handicap as meaning un-able;
2) the conceptualisation of the skills and knowledge to be mastered as an inflexible standard to be reached before independence can be awarded, and
3) because of the apparent desire to shield both the mentally handicapped person and society from each other.

The objectives/skills analysis approach and curriculum purports to teach the skills for independent living, but independence itself is not available because of the existence of 'mental handicap'. The control exerted over their lives, by others, means that they lack the opportunities to develop independence.

We are not suggesting that the tasks and skills children with severe learning difficulties are taught in school under the new orthodoxy are of no value, or that they may not be useful to the children, either now or in later life. What we are suggesting is that such an education does not add up to learning to be independent, to participating in and contributing to one's own community, either as a child or later as an adult, as the aims of education purport. Rather the objectives/skills analysis curriculum actually teaches dependence, in that it does not teach the children to challenge the system they are in and the places they will graduate to. The curriculum is not seen in terms of constant amelioration of handicapping conditions but rather in terms of making up for deficiencies which are constantly imputed to the child. The curriculum, as it is, functions to make children with severe learning difficulties as near normal as possible - the means to the end - not to enhance who they actually are.

The curriculum is not about challenging the conception others may have of a person as mentally handicapped, both within the special education system and the school, and outside of education, although it may challenge the degree of handicap imputed to the pupil. Rather, the curriculum is about fitting children with severe learning difficulties for life as mentally handicapped adults, unable and dependent - or 'planned dependence', as it is sometimes euphemistically referred to. The objectives/skills analysis approach is antithetical to the idea of independence as it is commonly understood - i.e. free from external control, self-governing, self-supporting. It teaches children to perform tasks as if they were tricks, under specific conditions of control, because of the preference given to being able to do things at the 'knowing-of' level (B. Smith et al. 1983), and to the acquisition of skills as end products.

There is no critical analysis of what independence actually means, and what it does, might or could mean to children with severe learning difficulties. The link between objectives - which define the skills and tasks to be taught - and aims, is simply assumed. The consequent vision of independence is narrow, to say the least, as reflected by the concentration on skills for self-help and socialisation in what are seen as social education programmes. It has been indicated by some people, that the lack of objectives for developing interactional skills, decision-making strategies, and being able to practise self-determination, self control and autonomy in the social setting of the class, is more to do with what is easy to teach, easy to control, and easy to present in the neat written format required by the new orthodox approach than to what constitutes quality education for children with severe learning difficulties. For example, in the report 'Curriculum Planning for the ESN(S) Child' (Crawford 1980), which followed a workshop that had concentrated exclusively on the skills analysis approach to curriculum development, it is noted that considerable difficulty was experienced:

> ... in defining social education as members wished to incorporate rather wide ranging concepts, such as interaction with others, good manners and courtesy, responsibility, social acceptance and self-image. They came to realise that, worthy as those abstractions were, they did not produce practical decisions about the content of the curriculum (S. Robbins in Crawford (ed) 1980, p. 68).

Instead it was decided to focus on what mentally handicapped people 'would need to know and be able to do in specific situations' (Ibid., p. 69). Hence the monopoly of behavioural objectives on the closed curriculum and emphasis placed on the imperative type of teaching strategy.

The objectives/skills analysis approach is implicitly claiming that discrete, albeit functional skills together constitute a passport to participation in the ordinary community, both from the view of how the child could meaningfully interact with the community, given his inabilities and deficiencies and how he could be capable of successful community participation. But the objectives/skills analysis approach is detrimental to children learning active thinking strategies, decision-making, interrelating and self-determination. It is in opposition to achieving the aim of independence, except in the sense of being able to perform functional skills without aid from another person, at a time required by external circumstances.

No doubt many would agree with us when we say that the present objectives/skills analysis curriculum does not make children with severe learning difficulties into independent adults, but the common reason given would be the children's own inabilities, their mental handicap.

We have suggested, however, that the present curriculum based on skills analysis, conflicts with the idea of independence as self-governing and is detrimental to its achievement. The conflict relates the fact that the aims of education are derived from ideals of what constitutes normality which are interpreted as referring to normality as a standard against which people are judged. It is as if there is some arbitrary level at which a person becomes 'normal' that is expressed in an ability to become an independent, participating and contributing member of the community at large - Warnock's criterion of educational success. The inherent assumption in the design of the objectives/skills analysis approach to education is that independence can be achieved if enough skills are learned, enough ticks amassed on the checklist, that is, if the child functions more normally. The criterion of the severity of handicap, within the special school itself, relates to the skills a child has, or could potentially acquire, and consequently how close his behaviour comes to being acceptable in terms of idealised norms.

By adhering to aims of education as the same for everyone, the present curriculum is in fact aiming at a particular level of competence in living which is associated with 'success' in the wider societal structure. Since mental handicap is, by definition, referenced against the criterion of normality, for children who also by definition do not reach that criterion, setting the aims of education within the reference framework of 'normality' ensures that the aims remain rhetorical, and bear little relation to practice, as in the case of the concept of 'independence'. Teaching discrete, functional skills creates normal appearances in performance, but does not challenge the labelling of the child with severe learning difficulties as a future mentally handicapped adult. The 'independence' taught by the objectives /skills analysis curriculum merely gives a grad- uated assessment against which the child may be seen to be more or less severely handicapped by his disability. No notion of the social construction of handicap is offered within the objectives/skills analysis approach and thus no means by which the child with severe learning dif- ficulties, the mentally handicapped adult to be, can challenge the conception of himself as 'mentally handicapped' with its restrictive and negative connotations.

The objectives/skills analysis curriculum aims at increasing independence, but 'autonomy' - the expression of independence within one's own life - is not being tackled by this curriculum. As far back as 1974, Cunningham wrote that:

> ... we all appear to aim for increasing independence for these children and adults, usually expressed in the teaching of social and self-help skills. However this does not necessarily provide autonomy. Many subnormal

people proficient in these skills are still highly dependent upon others for decision-making as to how they will live and for social and emotional support.

He goes on to ask:

... how much control do they have over their lifestyles, what decisions should they make, could they make, and do they make? Are we really educating them to make decisions? (Cunningham 1974, p. 50).

The educational programme ostensibly treats children with severe learning difficulties as different in its intense emphasis on functional skills. In so doing it is aiming not to provide an enabling environment based on the principle of normalisation i.e. making 'use of culturally valued means in order to enable people to live culturally valued lives' (Wolfensberger and Thomas 1981). Instead it is aiming to try and make children with severe learning difficulties look the same as ordinary children. It is <u>normalising them</u> in a manner which, for us, provides not for independence, but rather for a subtle form of dependence because it blames the child (the future mentally handicapped adult) for what has been socially constructed - namely the limitation of rights, opportunities and status. Furthermore, a lack of humanity is imparted to those who do not reach the required standards of being accepted as fully human, i.e. to be 'normal', self-supporting and conforming.

The objectives/skills analysis paradigm does not acknowledge that children with severe learning difficulties are valuable human beings in their own right, with abilities as well as inabilities, and with something to offer other people. It oppresses their value as first and foremost, people, like the rest of us, because its aims and content legitimate constant comparison with an idealised state of normality, the aspiration towards normal appearances as success, and the consequent emphasis upon deficits to be remedied. The present curriculum reaffirms the position of children with severe learning difficulties as mentally handicapped children, and therefore de-valued people, second class citizens, because of <u>their</u> inabilities.

CONTRADICTIONS AND PARADOX IN THE CURRICULUM FOR
CHILDREN WITH SEVERE LEARNING DIFFICULTIES: THE
INSTITUTIONALISATION OF DEPENDENCE

The curriculum associated with the objectives/
skills analysis paradigm defines education and
curriculum development in operational terms, without any examination of where the ideas utilised
came from and the assumptions upon which they are
based. The only justification given is in terms of
the 'specific' learning difficulties of mentally
handicapped children, and in terms of the 'need to
know where you are going'. The 'community' and
'mental handicap' are taken as given. For example,
it is generally considered that the main obstacle
to mentally handicapped adults holding down open
employment is their own handicap, not that the
employment system is primarily to blame for such
students not getting jobs. More fundamentally, it
is taken for granted that it is right and desirable
to increase the behavioural repertoire of children
with severe learning difficulties along very
specific lines, and decrease it along other
specific lines, without regard to any desires or
wants they may have of their own. This is coupled
with the possibility of utilising a methodology
which may not allow the child even the choice of
opting out, since this will be defined as
maladaptive.

The objectives/skills analysis curriculum is
based on specific beliefs, although these are not
made explicit. The paradigm represents a
particular way of looking at children with severe
learning difficulties and mentally handicapped
people, and puts forward a particular imperative as
to the aim and content of their education. In so
doing, it presents its view and imperative as self-
evident truths, emanating naturally (and neutrally)
from the specific learning difficulties of the
children concerned, and from their inclusion within
the education system as 'educable'. Our argument
is that what are taken as self-evident truths are
implicit assumptions about the nature of mental
handicap, the nature of society and the purpose and
constitution of education. These assumptions are
entrenched, firstly in the medical model of mental
handicap, and secondly in a conception of education
as worthwhile in what it results in, rather than
for its own sake. These assumptions are:
1) that mental handicap exists as an entity in its
own right. It consists of cognitive impairment(s)
and deficits, which result in learning difficulties

45

and abnormal learning patterns. These are responsible for socially incompetent and maladaptive behaviour;

2) that the mental handicap seriously impairs an individual's ability to live within the community independently;

3) that mental handicap is incurable, but that levels of functioning can be improved in terms of the performance of tasks. However, ability to interact with others, take responsibility for their own actions, and make decisions in a responsible manner, will always be seriously impaired in comparision with 'normal' people because of limited cognitive capacity;

4) that education should be predominantly a goal oriented activity;

5) that participation for mentally handicapped people within society, rather than on its periphery, is a matter of mentally handicapped people acquiring and acting in accordance with dominant cultural norms, and that as such the latter represent desirable goals of education;

6) that ends in education are more important than the means, and can be used to justify and legitimate the means;

7) that children with severe learning difficulties, and mentally handicapped people, require highly structured teaching for effective learning to occur, and that as such, the objectives model of pupil outcomes, together with behaviourist teaching techniques, represent the only successful and relevant approach to their education.

It might seem as if we are suggesting that the objectives/skills analysis paradigm represents some kind of conspiracy against mentally handicapped people. We are not. The assumptions embodied are implicit, veiled by unquestioned beliefs that 'education ... is a good, and a specifically human good, to which all human beings are entitled' (Warnock 1978 1:7) and that providing children with severe learning difficulties with practical skills is 'education'. This represents, at the very least, the nearest approximation to independence that mentally handicapped people can achieve. Many teachers working with the objectives/skills analysis paradigm obviously believe that they are systematically working towards independence, in so far as the children are capable of achieving it (e.g. Booth and Statham 1982).

Because the assumptions made about mental handicap and education are not made explicit, they

are not open to question or debate. Curriculum
development has not included the development of
educational theory and the rigorous questioning of
practice in relation to theory, and so has not
examined the implications of the value judgements
being made and the assumptions behind what is
actually being taught, and how. In fact there has
been a total lack of theory informing the practice
of education for these children, except at a
pragmatic level - what they need to know, and how
they need to be taught - as shown by 'scientific'
research about their deficits and learning
difficulties. There has been no debate about what
mental handicap or severe learning difficulty means
in terms of education; of what education means in
relation to mental handicap; what assumptions both
'mental handicap' and 'education' are based on;
what education should be for, what it should, could
or might consist of, how it could/should occur; and
WHY - in relation to all these questions. Instead,
the universality of the aims of education has been
taken for granted and the only purpose of
curriculum development has been to articulate the
path towards the achievement of those aims. As
Cunningham notes, the aims of education are:

> ... value judgements of what people we
> teach ought to be ... at the end of the formal
> educational process ... and ... the aims ...
> of education ... provide the source or start-
> ing point of the curriculum and help us decide
> what we should teach ... it is from precise
> objectives and measurements of learning that
> we gain the information for prescriptive
> teaching and realistically assess what can be
> taught (Cunningham 1974, p. 49).

Education as socialisation and developing
social competence, has unquestioningly been seen as
compatible with the overall purpose of education as
preparation for adulthood and personal development,
in terms of the needs and possibilities for
children with severe learning difficulties. Why
and how objectives relating to socialisation and
social competence should constitute progress
towards the overall purpose of education, and
whether conceiving of education as a means to a
specific end (which is the same for all children)
is constructive for mentally handicapped people,
are issues which have not been examined. Why such
a content is being taught, and the relationship to

47

aims of how objectives are taught, are issues which
have been side-stepped by the hierarchical, means-
end organisation of the curriculum. The question
'why' has always been answered in terms of the
universal aims of education and the position of
children with severe learning difficulties now as
being educable. Questions of 'how' are answered
simply in terms of providing the means towards the
end - however eventual that might be. The implicit
nature of assumptions being made by the objec-
tives/skills analysis approach and the lack of
critical analysis compound the situation. The
impression given is that there is only one major
approach to educating children with severe learning
difficulties; education and mental handicap are
commonly understood - education as a natural process and mental handicap as a natural state; that
there are no conflicts within this approach; and
there are no alternatives. That the present concept of educating children with severe learning
difficulties involves specific value judgements
about the abilities and inabilities of mentally
handicapped people and their status as human
beings, goes unrecognised.

The little published material which is
critical of the objectives/skills analysis paradigm
(McConkey 1981; B. Smith et al. 1983; Goddard
1983), or which attempts to analyse the meaning and
relationship of education and mental handicap from
a theoretical point of view, in the way in which
McMaster (1973) envisaged, does not, however,
explain alternatives in any detailed analysis. A
tentative start only is made by Serpell-Morris
(1982) and Goddard (1983). This lack of substantial criticism and alternatives contrasts sharply
with the copious number of articles and books which
put forward an objectives curriculum model and
utilise skills analysis for programme content.
Although behaviourism has long since been discounted as an adequate developmental theory (Sinha
1981), and although the objectives curriculum model
has been extensively criticised outside of the
field of mental handicap, (e.g. Stenhouse 1975),
the two, within the skills analysis paradigm, totally dominate the education of children with
severe learning difficulties. That there is a
recognised alternative curriculum model available -
the process model (Stenhouse 1975) - which emphasises processes within the educational enterprise
rather than the end products to be achieved, is not
acknowledged. Goddard (1983) specifically notes how

the work of Mildred Stevens (1976 and 1978), who emphasised the importance of processes in the education of children with severe mental handicap, has been, ' ... stifled by the "scientific" behaviourist approach' (Goddard 1983, p. 261).

Given this state of affairs, it is not surprising that many teachers appear to be unaware of the assumptions that they implicitly accept and adopt within the present orthodoxy and the subsequent implications for their teaching practice which ensure that they treat children with severe learning difficulties in a particular way - as mentally handicapped people. In so doing they also maintain the negatively valued concept of mental handicap and handicapping conditions because of the differentiation, discrimination and the valuing procedure which they are participating in, by referencing mental handicap against the standards of 'normality'.

The contradictions involved in practice, where 'personal development' and development for a specific future of fitting into the community are both held up as goals, are similarly hidden from view. Beresford et al.'s study (1982), for example, indicates the general lack of awareness and acknowledgement of the contradictions involved in the education of adolescents and young people with severe learning difficulties. Here, a liberal view of education as the development of the potential of each individual child is being espoused simultaneously with preparation for a particular adult role, inextricably connected to a stratified society where mentally handicapped people are at the bottom of the status ladder. They raise,

> ... the fundamental question of whether broad-based, individual-oriented education will ever be possible for mentally handicapped and other children and young adults as long as employment and the labour market are not orientated to the needs of the individual worker, workers collectively and the community (Beresford et al. 1982, p. 242).

The fact that personal development and the development of autonomy and self-determination may be incompatible with the strict behaviourist teaching techniques, is also not an issue which has been discussed in terms of curriculum development. Programmes for teaching self-control and choice through behaviourist techniques, (e.g. Kiernan 1981

and Kiernan et al. 1978) appear with no discussion
of the methodology for such content and no discussion of alternatives. Brennan makes note of the
idea that 'how you teach' may be as important a
'what you teach', in terms of eventual outcomes,
but states that in his experience the '... link
between methods and objectives was rarely discussed' (Brennan 1979, p. 75).

However, there is a way in which the present
orthodoxy is underlaid with another kind of 'taken
for grantedness', which occurs at a deeper level
than the ready acceptance of the objectives/skills
analysis approach as a highly suitable education
for children with severe learning difficulties.
This occurs in the structure of the day in school,
and in what counts as school knowledge. It means
that dependence is not simply a product of the
particular curriculum strategy now dominating the
education of these children. It means that
dependence is embedded in our very ways of working,
which pervade the curriculum through and through.

The structure of the day centres around
particular institutional events - dinner times,
play times, arrivals, departures - and around ideas
about when children and teachers are most alert and
receptive, as well as the availability of communal
rooms, the mini-bus or the swimming pool. Days are
divided up into segments according to timetables
which tend to reflect a very definite division
between work and play, or enrichment. Work is the
hard option, and usually takes place in the
morning. The softer options are for the afternoon,
when it can be arranged that way. Work-time is
when education specifically takes place, and
children are taught. It is synonymous with
children sitting down quietly (if they are mobile)
and completing tasks, either on their own or in a
One-to-One teaching situation with an adult. It is
when children will be working towards the individual objectives set by the teacher. Control and
conformity are its hallmarks. During the soft
options things happen like going out, 'creative'
activities, art, clay work, dancing, singing or
horse-riding. But these activities are seen not so
much as about teaching and learning important
skills, as about enjoying oneself, filling in time
in a reasonably pleasurable manner, whether for
teacher or pupils. There is more to-ing and fro-
ing, standing up and moving about, more noise, less
atmosphere of control.

This actually presents a real paradox. When

the teacher is teaching in work-time, the children
are controlled rigidly. They are treated in a
dependent manner, as recipients, respondents to
orders, requests, tasks to do, as the teacher
directs.   Education for children with severe
learning difficulties, is about 'vacuum ideology',
a label coined by sociologists to describe the
attitude that sees education as filling up empty
vessels - empty because of the children's deficits
and handicaps which means they haven't got the
relevant experiences and knowledge they should
have. The paradox lies with the teachers choosing
little bits of time in which they 'teach' independence - as skills - whilst contradicting the idea of
independence in the manner in which they behave.
The very way work-time is divided into specific
sessions for different things so that learning is
fragmented, and the skills are gained and practised
outside of their usual context, in artificial situations, is indicative of this paradox between what
represents dependence, but is supposedly about
learning independence. For example, undertaking an
undressing programme in the middle of the morning;
cleaning teeth and washing faces as soon as the
child gets to school; doing a 'John say please' or
'look at me' programme first thing in the morning
and rewarding the child with bits of sausage because that's what he likes and so on.
    Play is a case in hand in schools catering for
these children.   Free play is something that
happens on the periphery of things - first thing in
the morning as the teacher waits for all the
children to arrive; last thing in the morning as
the teacher clears up for dinner time; filling in
bits of the afternoon, or in the last session of
the afternoon. Free play takes up time and space
with the children doing things that the teacher
knows they can do. It legitimates and justifies
activities that merely 'occupy', under the guise of
'choice'. Play is not viewed as a medium through
which learning takes place; yet play is the work of
all children. It is the major means by which they
learn about themselves and their environment.
Because of their 'incidental learning deficit' it
is supposed that mentally handicapped children
cannot play in a constructive, spontaneous,
progressive manner so that they learn. They have
to be taught how to play and even then, this is
only in terms of being able to occupy themselves,
since their need for structured teaching in order
to learn all the other skills that they must

achieve if they are to progress, takes precedence -
during work-time. The authors have themselves
experienced situations where core curricula drawn
up for young children with severe learning
difficulties have not even mentioned 'play'.

The normative framework which pervades special
education for children with severe learning
difficulties seems to act as a kind of filter
through which everything is seen in schools. It
thereby acts as a means of transforming the
structural determinants of handicap so that they
are constituted in the everyday activities of
teachers and pupils. Normal standards are
continuously imposed during the course of the day
in the special school on situations and children
which are obviously not ordinary or normal, so that
in every possible way things look normal.
Frequently, the standards set are idealised, not
ordinary. The amount of 'sitting down at tables'
type of behaviour demanded of children with severe
learning difficulties illustrates the infiltration
of this attitude and the exaggeration of what is
thought to represent 'normal' behaviour, i.e. what
is seen as a physical manifestation of the ability
to behave normally. When this is expected of
children of six to nine years of age, let alone
children under five years of age, who are in an
ordinary school would spend a great deal of time
moving about, the paradox is exemplified. The idea
that a One-to-One situation, the child is only
paying attention when he is sat at a table and has
eye contact with the teacher, and that it is only
at this point that teaching and education can
begin, is yet another fallacy resulting from the
paradoxical imposition of idealised standards.

The significance of the normative framework is
further entrenched in what actually counts as
knowledge. For example, in teaching children to
communicate, the emphasis is upon the child
speaking (what is normative in communicating) and
if he cannot or will not speak then a recognised
signing system is introduced as the next best
thing. Even though the child will have his own
means of communication, either behavioural or
gestures, these are either ignored or every effort
is made to change his signs into standardised ones.
This is rather than having to teach other people to
recognise the child's individual signs.

In imposing normal standards of behaviour, the
curriculum is beset with rigidity in what is seen
to constitute education and what 'doing education'

consists of. Tasks are seen in a totally normative way - e.g. the thing to do with a ring stack is to put the rings on the stick in the right order; the thing to do with an inset puzzle is to put all the pieces in the right place. If a child, at the appropriate level of development, can't do a task, then the teacher will actually spend a great deal of time teaching the child exactly how to do the task in its correct fashion. Teachers are advised by programmes such as EDY to do this in a highly systematic way using task analysis and rewarding the child when he completes the steps correctly. The behavioural approach emphasises that this is an approach which has success inbuilt into it. However this is because the whole thing is so manipulated, controlled, rigid and inflexible that only one way to do the task successfully is acknowledged. The teacher goes on teaching the steps to do this until she has achieved it, counting any other kind of behaviour of the child's with the materials, as irrelevant, inappropriate and to be ignored. In this sense, self expression is not allowed for. It is almost viewed as inherently maladaptive - a 'raw' manifestation of mental handicap. Even in creative activities such as art, teachers normalise the products. The child's squiggles on the paper are used to make leaves, or butterflies on the frieze; or the outline of some recognised object is drawn for a child to make some mark in, or the outline is imposed on the child's creation afterwards. Even the question 'what are you drawing/painting?' pre- supposes nine times out of ten an answer in the normative framework - a house, a tree, Mummy.

Dependence is actually institutionalised within special schools.

The imposition of normal and idealised stan- dards on to what is obviously not normal, and the motivation and justification of this in terms of educating children with severe learning difficul- ties so that they may gain in personal development and development for independent living in the com- munity, is full of paradox and contradiction and involves unintended and unrecognised consequences because of the lack of awareness and critical ana- lysis of these elements. The lack of awareness and critical analysis itself seems to stem from the 'taken for grantedness' of the goodness of educa- tion; of what education is or isn't without ever going into it in any depth; of what it means to educate, to teach, to learn; what children with severe learning difficulties should do and be to succeed; and of what appropriate knowledge is.

The present situation, in which the educational programme generated within the objectives/skills analysis paradigm is unquestioningly accepted as 'education' when its theoretical base is not advanced even by its proponents, exemplifies a dichotomous relationship between theory and practice. As Goddard comments, in the present climate of behavioural objectives and teaching packages, ' ... there is a very real danger that curriculum development as such could cease' (Goddard 1983, p. 251).

Even the research evidence about the particular characteristics of mentally handicapped children, and therefore their special educational needs, exist in a 'taken for granted' way so that the possibility of there being alternative ways in which to structure educational environments, apart from the objectives/skills analysis approach, is not recognised or acknowledged. The fact that everyday experience tells you that these children DO learn incidentally from what is going on around them (for example, how to attract attention, how to get at people, get out of things) is ignored. McConkey (1981) describes, for example, how a group of infants with Down's Syndrome learned the task of ring stacking experientially when left to their own devices, although they did take much longer than one little girl who was taught the task in the orthodox fashion of concentrating exclusively on the end product to be achieved. However the children who learned experientially generalised their skills to other tasks more quickly than the little girl, who had been taught.

As Swann points out, all events have a structure, and particular structures must be argued for as opposed to others. The structured teaching of the objectives/skills analysis paradigm rather sets itself up as the only alternative to what it infers are unstructured environments - or enrichment experiences. As Swann notes, '... the question of the kinds of structure that are conducive to mental, bodily and spiritual growth is sidestepped by the orthodoxy, and artificially buttressed by the mirage of achievement measured by behaviour' (Swann in Goddard 1983, p. 274).

However, the most disturbing aspect of the present orthodoxy in the education of children with severe learning difficulties is its simplistic acceptance of the concepts of mental handicap and education as given, and its misguided logic of objectives in relation to these concepts. As Goddard notes it gives, 'the illusion that we know precisely what we are about' (Goddard 1983, p. 251).

McMaster (1973) believed that educational theory could lead to a realistic appraisal of education for mentally handicapped people. The objectives/ skills analysis approach parades its educational programme as if it has concluded the theoretical debate concerning what education for children with severe learning difficulties should be about, when it hasn't even considered the question in anything but a shallow way and only from the narrow perspective of developmental psychology. The result is an approach which has little, if any, educational significance for these children. Rather, education is reduced to training and the rhetoric of independence for children with severe learning difficulties and mentally handicapped people is a sham. Despite their 'education', they remain dependent and consequently devalued people.

Chapter Three

TEACHING - RELATIONS AND PROCESSES OF IMPOSITION

Broad definitions and rules exist about the roles and activities involved in teaching and learning in schools. Schools are the formal organisations where the process of compulsory education occurs. Teachers are empowered by the State to be the agents of education in schools, and pupils are recipients of education, there to learn.

The roles of teacher and pupil are now institutionalised within the compulsory education system as mutually exclusive functions - the teacher teaches and the pupil learns. Although it is obvious, it is important to note that from the outset, schools formally place teachers in a position of power over children, in order that comparatively few adults (i.e. teachers) can teach a large number of children (i.e. pupils).

The level at which it is taken for granted that there is a common understanding of the role of the teacher, and the role of the pupil, in the education of children with severe learning difficulties, is perhaps indicated by the total lack of any analysis and discussion of the teacher-pupil relationship which goes beyond 'tips for teachers'. Even though presentations may sometimes give the appearance of more than this, by centring on generalised issues, such as the skills needed by teachers of children with severe learning difficulties, or teacher training, analysis is virtually always at the level of how to teach and how to decide what to teach. What teaching might be, apart from, instead of, or as well as this finite conglomeration of skills (shaping, fading, chaining, demonstrating, presenting visual aids, verbal cues, prompts) is not questioned or debated. What the role of pupil constitutes, or what learning is, is seen as even less problematic. The only recognised difficulty is in ensuring that the child is ready to be taught and can therefore learn appropriately. For example, if he does not pay attention, look at the teacher, listen to the teacher, then he needs a 'paying attention' programme. What teaching and learning mean per se is in this way taken as given.

Within wider circles, there is some analysis of what teaching should, or should not be. For example, that teaching should not be indoctrination is argued vehemently in the philosophy of education, by the Department of Education and Science, and the mass media especially when there is some controversy about particular subject matter and approaches to it (e.g. the case of 'Peace Studies' in 1984 in secondary schools). On the other hand, it is clear that most people would agree that teachers in the school should play a part in socialising children, that is, inculcating behaviour associated with dominant values in society such as being polite, treating other people respectfully, and abiding by the law.

The teacher's position relates to being both 'in authority', because of the legal procedures binding the education system and the rules and regulations of individual schools and local education authorities; and 'an authority' in that she is a person professionally trained to do the job. The teacher's own authority in the class, further relates to things like her own personality and charisma, as well as to her adult status, her performance in class and the pupils' views of it. Similarly, the pupil's subordinate position relates not simply to their legal status as pupils, but also their status as children and the lack of maturity, experience, knowledge and skills with which that status is usually associated. That children have a need for education to be able to cope with and participate in our society, is implicit in the compulsory nature of schooling.

However, if teaching is to be concerned with educating and not simply training, and certainly not indoctrination, then pupils must voluntarily accept the teacher's authority and must play something of an active role in the proceedings. In mainstream schools it is virtually impossible to conceive of teachers being able to compel children to learn what it is deemed they should, without some kind of active co-operation on their part. Sheer numbers suggest this, let alone the pupils awareness of their ability to disrupt lessons, to fool about and find ways around doing what they have been asked.

In the education of children with severe learning difficulties, however, the issues of what is education, rather than training or indoctrination, and the importance of the pupil voluntarily accepting the teacher's authority, are not so clear cut. We have already described the dominant trends in the content of the educational programme for these children, as being concerned with social competence and socialisation, which many people would think of in terms of training, rather than education. The retort is, of course, that this represents education for children with severe learning difficulties because it is catering for their needs. It is education at their level. The position is complicated by the pupils' lack of independence, their inabilities, which comprise their very need for special education. Not only is the child with severe learning difficulties in a subordinate position because of his place as a pupil, but also because of the way teaching for independence is institutionalised in a manner which embodies dependent relationships between the teacher and the pupil.

Teachers in schools catering for these children are continually surrounded by an environment which defines the pupils as dependent. The dependence of the children is not only institutionalised in the way the day is structured within the classroom, and the way the content of the curriculum is presented, it is actually built into the structure of the school as an organisation and the roles children and teachers are expected to fulfill within that organisation. For example, these children are almost inevitably bussed into school on special buses, or else in taxis with their own escorts; the school day is significantly shorter than in ordinary schools, often not beginning until 9.30 a.m. or 10.00 a.m. when all the pupils in the class have finally arrived, and ending between 3.00 and 3.30 p.m. so that the transport can get them home again, either before the traffic gets too heavy, or in a reasonable amount of time since many have long distances to travel; the lunch break is longer - one and a half to two hours - often ostensibly to allow time for feeding difficulties of some children, and to cover all the staff members breaks. These kinds of occurences in schools do not necessarily happen because the pupils <u>are</u> dependent and unable.

Rather it is more frequently a matter of expediency for the ease of administration and organisation. The overall impression created and the expectations aroused, however, are in relation to the dependence of the pupils on others, their inabilities and their low level of functioning.

Inside the building itself locks abound - on cupboards, in classrooms and hallways, where equipment can be kept out of reach, or access prevented to that which might cause a nuisance or danger. For example classroom doors may be locked to keep children in at lesson times, and out when they are supposed to be elsewhere. Where there aren't locks, there are security handles at the tops of doors where the children can't reach them.

Playgrounds are designed and arranged to minimise risks - not too many hiding places, little play equipment available and usually a clear view to the perimeters so that those on duty can keep watch relatively easily. Some, of course, have ten foot high fences, and locked gates, not to mention the inbuilt reflex of an experienced teacher or dinner lady to continually count heads. Mainstream schools, too, have locks, bars and fences, but nowadays this tends to signify a desire to keep others out, rather than necessarily to keep the children in.

Special schools, just like mainstream schools, have their own rules and routines, which involve a fair amount of regimentation and inflexibility in allowing the institution to run reasonably smoothly, and for all needs, including those of the institution, to be met. This is obviously necessary to some degree, when a large number of children are being looked after by comparatively few adults, but it can often mean that the institution's rules and routines, ostensibly there to cater for its needs, over-ride the 'needs' of individual pupils. For example a teacher may find that she is unable to provide dinner for a particular child, in the classroom, even though she feels the child needs a quiet and undisturbed atmosphere in which to carry out a feeding programme, because the rule of the school is to eat in the dining room only and at the appointed time (for whatever reason).

There is a way in which meeting the child's special educational needs is translated into individualised programmes which take place at designated times, or only in the confines of the individual's classroom, rather than taking place across the whole spectrum of school life, since in the last instance the needs of the institution supercede those of individual children. Furthermore, as began to emerge from our discussion about the curriculum, there is a way in which children's needs may actually be identified in terms of the needs of the institution. Conformity to routine, regulations and rules appears in this way to be a major need of the institution, further institutionalising dependence, in the form of regimentation and control.

In these kinds of ways, dependence is actually institutionalised in the very nature of special schools which have been designed and are run to cater for these children's needs, en bloc. Everything around teachers of children with severe learning difficulties defines their pupils as dependent, unable, irresponsible, immature, not to be trusted.

Within this kind of atmosphere, what counts as 'educating', rather than training or indoctrination, becomes merely an academic exercise in the philosophy of education. It appears to bear little relevance to the difficulties and dilemmas teachers are faced with in carrying out their daily tasks, sometimes with pupils who may overtly show very few or very limited signs, if any, of voluntary responses. Perhaps these factors begin to explain why, '... Little attention is now given to developing interaction and self-regulatory behaviour and considerable emphasis is placed on the imperative type of teaching strategy' (B. Smith et al. 1983, p. 23). In the latter the concentration in teaching is 'almost exclusively on products and outcomes' (McConkey 1981, p. 9), achieving desired results, rather than on processes, sharing knowledge and developing understanding, and allowing children to extend means of self-determination and autonomy.

Our argument is that teacher-pupil relations, in the education of children with severe learning difficulties, are dominated by relations of imposition, where these children are required to learn in a prescribed way, without regard to their views or desires, and narrowing their options within situations to such an extent that they have no viable alternative to compliance. In our view, teaching as imposition does not represent education. Furthermore, such relations of teaching amplify the role of children with severe learning difficulties as dependent people, devalued, discriminated against and thereby handicapped.

PROFESSIONALISED TEACHING FOR CHILDREN WITH SEVERE LEARNING DIFFICULTIES - THE CREATION AND MAINTENANCE OF HANDICAPPING CONDITIONS

Too often, and too easily the education offered to children with severe learning difficulties is imposition, when the child's point of view is not taken into account, and he is placed in situations where others, apart from himself, control the opportunities, the interaction and the responses. As we have indicated, the objectives/ skills analysis approach to the curriculum treats the pupil as a deficit system, and the one with the 'problem'. The teacher is the person with the answers as far as education goes. The traditional teaching role of teacher as 'an authority' and 'in authority', back up the teacher's position as an 'expert' in any teaching situation. But other factors at work in special education enhance the teacher's authority, to the point of teaching as imposition being seen as the appropriate teaching strategy, both by practitioners in today's schools and by those who train or advise them. Teaching as imposition is seen as legitimate and justified because of the children's difficulties and deficits - their needs. The children's 'immaturity', their 'inability' to understand the rationale behind such things as conventions of polite behaviour, for example, are cited as part of the legitimation and justification of imposing learning on them, since, like very young children, they are unable to know their own best interests or their own minds.

Within the teaching situation the child has already been identified as a child with a problem. His severe learning difficulties are seen to represent special educational needs which result, inevitably, in his position in the special education system. In providing special education to meet the special educational needs of these children, there is little, if any separation of the different elements which either may be required, or are in fact present in the provision of special education in special schools or units. Special teaching (e.g. low teacher-pupil ratios), special education (e.g. content, curriculum), and special environments (e.g. segregated schools or units and specific types of organisation), are all involved in the provision of special education for children with severe learning difficulties. All these incorporate particular implications for the management of the school as an institution, the teacher's role, and the teacher-pupil relationship. Rather than the child's needs being related to specific requirements connected to these distinct issues, the emphasis is laid upon the teacher, as the person designated to deal with the child's problems, and help him by providing the special education necessary on a daily basis to meet his special educational needs.

As the label 'severe learning difficulties' suggests, in educational terms the most significant characteristics of the children are their learning difficulties. Brennan gives the kind of lengthy listdescribing 'slow learners' which is typical of the way children with special educational needs are viewed in terms of their deficits and the implications these are assumed to have for education. Children with severe learning difficulties are seen to have more of the same characteristics:

> ... low level of intellectual competence; gross perceptual immaturity; restricted language; marked personal and social immaturity; difficulty with concept formation; difficulty with sequential thought; extreme difficulty in establishing new knowledge or skills; severe difficulty with learning in basic school subjects; low level of general awareness; and continually shifting attention and interest (Brennan 1979, p. 150).

In addition to the above, 'severe learning difficulties' are also associated with: - lack of spontaneous learning, lack of imagination and powers of abstraction, extreme difficulties in all but the simplest communications, lack of intrinsic motivation to learn from and explore the environment, inability to distinguish dangers by self, and an inability to concentrate except for short periods. Since such difficulties are noted as deficits against the norm, it appears logical and 'natural' that, in the main, definitions of children's 'needs' are based around difficulties and deficits. The assumption that follows from the perception of the children as deficit models, is that in order to combat their difficulties (their difference from the norm), the children need expert help, both in terms of what they are taught (as we have discussed in Chapters One and Two), and how.

The teacher who works with children with severe learning difficulties is seen as the expert in their education - a 'professional' person. She has (or is presumed to have) a specific body of knowledge about the learning difficulties of these children - their deficits, their problems; about teaching methodology - how to get them to learn; and about what it is they 'need' to learn. As such, she is thought of as having a deep understanding of the subject of education for children with severe learning difficulties and has expertise in practising in their education - that is, in teaching.

The particular expertise of such a teacher is presented by the literature in the field and within full-time and in-service training, as comprising of specific professional skills. For example, according to Mittler (1981) the professional teacher of children with severe learning difficulties, both now and in the future, should be able to offer, within the classroom, a number of particular skills, on top of basic classroom skills of management and organisation. These include being able to use individual assessment measures; accurately record observations of children's behaviour; specify behavioural objectives; use proficiently task analysis, prompting, shaping, chaining, reinforcing and generalisation techniques; and design, implement and evaluate individual programmes, utilising all such skills.

These particular skills essentially delineate the teacher's role in the terms of the objectives/skills analysis paradigm, and therefore in terms of the imperative to operationalise the particular view of education for children with severe learning difficulties embodied in that approach (Mittler 1981; Brennan 1973; Gardner et al. 1983; Kiernan 1981; Roberts 1982). Gardner et al.'s 'Skills Analysis Model' (1983) goes as far as stating categorically that behavioural methods of teaching are required in order to make the most effective use of the intensive One-to-One teaching necessitated by their curriculum model. In this way, the methodology required defines the teacher's role in the classroom. They present no other discussion of the role of the teacher, the teacher-pupil relationship or the relations of teaching, which are implied.

The only other kinds of sentiments which are discussed in relation to the teacher's 'professionalism', and her role in teaching children with severe learning difficulties, are words either exhorting her to be enthusiastic, dedicated and committed, or praising her for such personal qualities. Such qualities are themselves seen in relation to the extra or different skills required by teachers for children with severe learning difficulties, as compared to teachers of ordinary children (Staff of Rectory Paddock School 1981; Pamphlet 60 DES 1975; Brennan 1973) The Staff of Rectory Paddock School summarise the kinds of competence required in future from teachers of these children as: - curricular planning and organisation, record keeping, diagnostic teaching (i.e. teaching based on assessing children's needs in terms of what they can't do), and awareness of research. They go on:

> But what about personal qualities? Special school teachers ... are frequently praised by laymen for being "dedicated"; in future if such a compliment is to be earned, it must indicate a truly professional level of dedication, with absolute commitment - never letting up, never relaxing our efforts, never indulging our personal whims at the expense of the children's education.

> All this may be a lot to ask, but how can we settle for doing less? If the mentally handicapped child could express his condition in poetry he ... might well have written, especially for us, the words - "... if you do not teach me I shall not learn ..." (Staff of Rectory Paddock School 1981, p. 97).

The thrust towards using highly systematic and structured teaching has placed the teacher (at least ideally, if not at present practically in all schools) in the role of employing a supposed scientific pedagogy - i.e. based on scientific principles and on methods of teaching and learning established as correct and successful by research. The adoption of a scientific pedagogy has been taken as enhancing the professionalism of teachers of children with severe learning difficulties. This is significant in the light of the fact that they have only been recognised as 'teachers' as such, for the last decade and a half. It enhances the position of the teacher as an 'expert' in her own field. It also expresses, however, in educational terms the professional-client relationship based on the medical model of personal illness and treatment. For example Brennan suggested in 1973, that:

> ... teachers who are to deal with the severely subnormal child need to act more deliberately; they have to impose the structure with much more care; they have to be able to work out the curriculum in much more detail. They have to be able to state, not only the general aims of education, but the behavioural objectives necessary for the achievement of those aims, in terms of the knowledge to be acquired, the skills to be established, the attitudes which would be beneficial, and the values to be promoted. And to state these in behavioural terms which are capable of assessment and measurement during the process of education, so that outcomes can be fed back into the teaching situation, which becomes a continually diagnostic one (Brennan 1973, p. 25).

This 'scientific pedagogy' is methodology informed specifically by psychological theories and research. It has grown up amongst the practice of diagnosis, classification and remediation of mental handicap and other impairments (deafness, blindness, and physical handicap), that stemmed from the emergence of disabled people as a social problem and a cause for social concern, particularly during the Nineteenth Century. As Sinha points out, psychology and special education emerged together:

> ... not only did psychological theories underpin special education practices, but the 'subjects' of special education provided the subject matter for the emerging specialisation of developmental and child psychology.

Now: ... the relationship is institutionalised in myriad organisational, administrative and ideological forms; the conceptual tools at the teacher's disposal, and the vocabulary in which the curricular objectives are set - discrimination, cognitive development, reinforcment, motor skills - are those of psychology (Sinha 1981, p. 402).

Teachers of children with severe learning difficulties have inherited this long tradition

within special education. Furthermore, the concept
of mental handicap itself was engendered by medical
officers and psychologists. During the years of
'ineducability', mentally handicapped children and
adults were always seen to be the responsibility of
the medical and psychological professions. Work
with mentally handicapped people has been primarily
undertaken under the guise of medicine, health
care, and psychology. Where training and education
took place, it was for its therapeutic benefits.
The body of knowledge that exists about mental
handicap since the beginnings of the first
specialised institutions in the Nineteenth Century,
was, and still is primarily medical and
psychological.

At present then, the rhetoric of special
education suggests that it is the children's <u>needs</u>,
i.e. their learning difficulties, which require
their teachers to be competent in a specific
methodology associated with the objectives/skills
analysis approach, and to also have the personal
qualities which will enable them to carry out the
chosen approach with unflagging determination and
unhesitant attitude, for the children's sakes. The
teacher's role is encompassed by the imperative for
the child to acquire desired skills. The teacher's
professional skills sum up how this is to be
achieved via the teacher-pupil relationship
engendered when the teacher begins to carry out her
duty to ensure that the child learns what has been
prescribed.

Both the teacher's role and the teacher-pupil
relationship are shot through with the medical
model in the guise of psychological concepts and
terminology, which have become so pervasive that
teachers use them as if they are 'natural', 'self
evident' and neutral.

What is happening is that the role of the
teacher is being defined as that of the treatment
officer. The subsequent teacher-pupil relationship
is a professional-client relationship.

Children's deficits, in comparison to the norm
(what they can't do) are understood as their
special educational 'needs'. These 'needs' are
then translated into deficits in learning - what
the child hasn't learned or that the child has
learned the wrong behaviour. The educational
programme is about teaching appropriate behaviour
under the guise of teaching for individual needs,
so that now the word 'need', in terms of special
education, is often simply a euphemism. The

perceived deficiency is located within the child who is seen as the possessor of a collection of problems. The answer to the problems is seen to lie with the professionals, and the expertise they have in treating the child's problems, not with the child himself, his peers, significant others, the environment, or political, social or economic factors. Although all these may be viewed as adding to problems, or framing their expression in particular ways, they are not <u>the</u> answer to 'making the children better'.

The children's supposed special educational needs, and the belief that the teacher is a professional, an expert in her field, provide the justification, motivation and legitimation of teaching as imposition. Behaviour modification programmes provide the most obvious examples of teachers imposing what they have decided should be taught, upon the child, when carried out without the child's willing consent, seeking to change his behaviour in ways defined by the teacher. This conception of teaching, contains within it, the basic assumption of the professional-client relationship that, 'you will be better because I, the professional know better' (McKnight 1977, p. 30).

The way that teaching is now delineated for children with severe learning difficulties has concrete effects upon the teacher's position with regard to the child, the teacher-pupil relationship, what the teacher does in that position in the name of teaching, and how she does it.

Grossly Unequal Power Relations

The teacher-pupil relationship, as the professional-client relationship, takes on grossly unequal power relations. The teacher is in a position of being able to define what is deficient with regard to 'educational' capabilities in any particular case which she is responsible for. Teaching children with severe learning difficulties therefore involves teachers in defining children's 'needs' in terms of day-to-day education, and puts them in the position of being able to decide what is inappropriate, what is appropriate, what is effective and what counts as success. The teacher can define the situations in her terms, without regard to any wants, desires or feelings of the child. As McKnight notes:

> There is no greater power than the right to
> define the question. From that right flows a
> set of necessary answers. If the servicer can
> effectively assert the right to define the
> appropriate question, he has the power to
> determine the need of his neighbour, rather
> than meeting his neighbour's need (McKnight
> 1977, p. 31).

The specific teaching techniques deemed suitable
and effective for children with severe learning
difficulties give the teacher ample means of using
this power in terms of effectively imposing
learning on children, together with the
legitimation of the use of that power in the terms
of the children's 'needs'. Actions which would be
unthinkable in other parts of the education system
are not only allowed, but argued to be therapeutic
for children with severe learning difficulties.
Recourse to the medical model of mental handicap,
with teachers as 'experts' and education as
treatment, legitimates actions not otherwise
justifiable in terms of 'education'. For example,
'time-out' is commonly practised with children with
severe learning difficulties who are also disturbed
or disruptive, using sometimes, bare, locked, dark
rooms with unprotected walls. Other techniques of
restraint used under the guise of teaching these
children appropriate behaviours, include putting
arm splints on, not for physiological reasons, but
to stop them throwing things, or hitting other
children, or indulging in self-stimulatory
behaviours; and tying children on to chairs when it
is importune for them to remain seated, such as in
assembly. Another favourite is withholding food,
or taking food away at mealtimes, supposedly as a
means of teaching them correct mealtime behaviours.
All such measures are seen as techniques for
teaching children with severe learning difficulties
the appropriate behaviours. In the literature the
behaviourists strictly deny that such measures are
or should be used as punishments, or because they
make it easier for the teacher to cope with
difficult behaviour. Such measures are carried out
in the name of education, but it is difficult to
see any other meaning of education in these circumstances other than treatment of maladaptive
behaviour.
The vastly unequal relations of power are also
involved in the isolation of pupils, and the
implicit discouraging of any collective action on

the pupil's part, by the emphasis on individual programmes and One-to-One teaching. The pre-eminent place of One-to-One teaching in the classroom further separates children, who frequently act in isolation anyway, and the intense level of supervision necessitated by the implementation of the objectives/skills analysis approach must further deter any collective action which might seriously threaten the teacher's control.

The Prominence of the Disabling Professions

The influence of the medical model of mental handicap in the provision of special education, can further be seen in the way other professionals - paramedical staff - are involved. These professionals look after specific bits of the children in the school. The Speech Therapist, the Occupational Therapist, the Physiotherapist, and increasingly Art/Drama/Music Therapists, are responsible for 'servicing' particular parts of the child and his functioning, not to mention the educational psychologist's reign over all the behaviours people want to get rid of. As McKnight remarked about the 'disabling professions' - particularly medicine, health care, and education:

> As the systems are a set of managed parts, so the client is necessarily understood and processed as a set of manageable parts, each with its own service mechanic. These complex service systems remind one of those table mats in some restaurants that show a cow divided into parts locating the steak, the roast, the ribs and the tongue.

> In a like manner, professionalised service definitions increasingly translate need in terms of people in pieces (McKnight 1977, p. 29).

At the very least, such a way of viewing the child is dehumanising and devaluing. It also deflates the child's capabilities to act for himself in his own way, and maintains a disintegrated view of him as a set of different, though related problems. The child is not perceived as a whole person for whom education is a continual, integrated process.

The Emphasis on Conformity to a Normative and Idealised Model of Behaviour

The emphasis on conformity to required end

products, further entails the danger of the child's self-initiated activity not being accepted as part of his contribution to the educational enterprise. Instead it tends to be interpreted within the pathological conception of mental handicap as indicative of, or causing severe learning and behavioural difficulties, which themselves are seen to represent mental handicap. Within this frame of reference, it is likely that children's behaviours and activities which differ from those the teacher requires for what she sees as successful learning, will be defined as maladaptive. For example, lack of eye contact; the child's spontaneous movement around the room; playing with food; or using conventional equipment supplied by the teacher in a non-conventional way, such as using pieces of jigsaw puzzle to build a tower. Subsequently, the omnipotent programme can be brought into play and used to combat the child's supposedly 'maladaptive' behaviours. As such, the child's range of options are seriously curtailed. As it is, certain actions of children with severe learning difficulties warrant immediate responses from adults, whereas this would not be the case in mainstream education. For example, the child cannot play truant. If he walks out of school, he is an absconder. Neither are these children usually allowed to settle differences of opinion, e.g. over equipment, for themselves. Adults intervene to ensure that everything is settled fairly and amicably.

Dependence as the Basic Characteristic of the Teacher-Pupil Relationship

The emphasis upon teacher decision and pupil inability therefore entails establishing dependence, rather than independence, as the characteristic relation of the child to the teacher. The teacher-pupil relationship is about teacher control, teacher definition of 'needs' and criteria of acceptability of performance, and teacher evaluation of the teaching/learning experience. Since the influence of the medical model of mental handicap maintains that children's behaviours are both symptoms and cause, the cure being 'normalisation' - making more normal - the latter then represents the teacher's raison d' être. The imposition of normal appearances then becomes a significant criterion of the success within the means-end conception of education. When the teacher's control constantly over-rides the child's self-initiated actions, or the teacher construes them as 'disruptive' and signs of 'disturbance', preferring still, quiet, occupied children, passivity and dependence on the teacher result.

The adherence to the imperative type of teaching strategy is a direct reflection of this line of thinking, providing the teacher with a ready-made way of coping reasonably successfully, in terms of creating normal appearances, out of what may well appear to be vastly abnormal responses from the children. Directly telling the children what to do and how, or teaching them in such a manner that the options open to them are minimised is a way of almost ensuring that the correct, conformist response is invoked (as is the case in all behavioural methods - e.g. task analysis, shaping, chaining which involve presenting tasks so that children either do what is required or not, in strict black and white terms, there being no grey areas). It also ensures dependency and passivity on the part of the pupil in his own education.

The dependent relations between pupils and teachers, encouraged by the present view of professional teaching for children with severe learning difficulties, and the dominance of the medical model in delineating the problem and answer to the education of these children, are contradictory to the aims of education as independence and autonomy. This is especially so when aims are considered to be what teachers should be continually striving for, rather than end states in education. When aims are seen as idealistic end states, as they are at present in the education of children with severe learning difficulties, then any means towards them becomes justifiable, as is now the case. The teacher is in the role of treatment officer for a sick child. The role of the teacher as an expert, in control in the classroom, complements the objectives/skills analysis approach to the curriculum, as indeed it is meant to. The way the needs of the children are defined puts the teacher in the position of the vehicle through which the imperative to provide 'skills' is implemented and imposed on the child. This deficit and remediation model of special education fits into the utilitarian and instrumental concept of education, the traditional view of teaching as imparting, and the idea of special education helping to make children with severe learning difficulties more normal, useful and acceptable. Professionalised teaching of skills to plug up children's supposed deficits is the result.

Devaluation of the Child with Severe Learning Difficulties

The sum of the effects of the above (the way the teacher's role is delineated, and what then constitutes 'teaching') for the children, is that they are subjected to dehumanising and devaluing experiences which deny their rights as people, and debase the contributions they have to make. Furthermore, children's abilities to act for themselves are actually deflated especially when these represent to the teacher undesirable or unacceptable behaviours.

The present dominant teacher role and pupil-teacher relations do not represent 'education', if this is to be more than training and different from indoctrination. As Hirst and Peters maintain, respect for persons - particularly school pupils in this case - is a requirement of teaching if it is to represent education rather than training, or more crucially in this case, imposition. They suggest that:

> To show lack of respect for persons, is, for instance, to ignore his point of view when we use him purely for our own purposes, or to settle his destiny for him without taking account of his views about it, or to treat him purely as the occupant of a role by ignoring his more general status as a rational being.

For respect to be shown,

> ... he must not be regarded merely in his role as a learner ... or as a potential performer who can be equipped with a repertoire of skills (Hirst and Peters 1970, p. 92).

It seems to us that Hirst and Peters' indications of a lack of respect for people in the teaching situation aptly describe current practice in the education of children with severe learning difficulties.

If teacher-pupil relations in the education of these children do not involve respect for the pupil as a valuable person in his own right, with a point of view and the right and ability to make decisions given the opportunities - we maintain they do not in the present orthodox view of teaching children with severe learning difficulties, and the teacher's role - the teacher-pupil relationship and teaching itself are dehumanising, devaluing and discriminating for the child. As such, intellectual impairments are not being worked with and disabilities circumvented. Rather, teachers are assisting in handicapping children by their attitudes and practice. The medical conception of mental handicap as an entity in its own right, which results in abnormality and dependence, is determining the qualities of each person in the teaching relationship as 'professional' and 'client'. The professionalism of the teacher in special education has inflated these relations. The concept is one of handicapping help, not teaching for special needs.

PRESSURES, CONFORMITY AND IMPOSITION

It may have appeared to the reader that we are making teachers out to be ogres, special schools to be prisons, and what goes on in them as all inherently bad. However, we are not trying to suggest that all teachers of children with severe learning difficulties consciously and intentionally treat these children in dehumanising, discriminating and devaluing ways in the course of their teaching. Nor are we trying to suggest that there is some conspiracy among teachers to maintain the dependence of the individuals in their charge so they may protect their jobs and safeguard their own status as experts and very special people because they work with the 'mentally handicapped'.

For a start, there are many teachers struggling to make sense of what is happening in special education, and within it to maintain positive relationships with pupils that are not dehumanising to either party. Secondly, the majority of teachers we know who work with children with severe learning difficulties, are not nasty people who get a kick out of their power over the children. Rather, they have sincere intentions of helping mentally handicapped people, they enjoy their company and do think of them as individual personalities, and not simply as a set of symptoms.

Although we have pinpointed examples of practice which we feel are inherently dehumanising and devaluing for the child, we as teachers and individuals, are far more concerned with raising questions about the whole way teaching is viewed for children with severe learning difficulties, and the models and advice teachers are being given as

73

exemplary teaching practice. We are not interested in indulging in 'teacher-bashing' for its own sake. We feel that the present circumstances allow teachers few alternatives to teaching as imposition. In contrast considerable pressures are being placed on teachers of children with severe learning difficulties to act as experts who directly control the classroom situation and children's learning, in the manner that makes teaching imposition.

The movement towards, and research supporting the delineation of highly structured and systematic teaching, as being what children with severe learning difficulties require if they are to learn effectively, has obviously been very influential in persuading teachers to take up the predominant behaviourist, and so called 'scientific' methodology, in the major areas of the timetable and curriculum concerned with mastery of skills and control of behaviour. Specifying behavioural objectives in the main areas of development for individual children, and then working through strict, precise programmes designed so that the individual child should achieve the objectives, now represent the popular conception of what teaching is, for children with severe learning difficulties.

Underlying the 'special' skills of the teacher of children with severe learning difficulties, and her teaching role as implementer of the object-ives/skills analysis approach to the curriculum, are the pressures for the teacher to be seen to be effective, and to be teaching in the traditional sense of imparting knowledge. The idea that the teacher has to be seen to be in control to allow 'teaching' to take place, is still firmly entren-ched, and the common sense indications of being in control - quiet, obedient children being busily occupied by tasks - are still held as important criteria of whether or not teaching, and by impli-cation, education and learning, are taking place.

Pressure on the teacher to conform to the idea of teaching as being seen to be in control, may come from all sides - from other staff, the headteacher (depending on their definition of a 'good' teacher), from the Local Education Authority, the Inspectorate and Advisory Service (especially for teachers in their probationary year), from parents, who wish education to be firm and produce observable and desired results, which guide their children nearer to normality.

Maintenance of the teacher's status as a

'professional' with a specific sphere of expertise and knowledge, also becomes a potential issue when other professionals - Speech Therapists, Physiotherapists, Occupational Therapists - are increasingly being brought into the realm of special education, and are actually being involved with education in the classroom. The power of parents, as consumers, to question the teaching practice for their children, has also been extended, through parent workshops, parent help in school and the position of parent governors. The development and adherence to 'scientific pedagogy' adds a further layer of professionalism to the position of the teacher of children with severe learning difficulties.

The pressure to be seen to be a teacher, both in terms of efficacy in organisation and control in the classroom, and in implementing the desired curriculum successfully, is further related to the movement towards accountablity of teachers; the issue of efficiency in teaching, especially in terms of meeting individual needs; and the question of relevance of education to pupil's needs. The general moves towards a core curriculum for all pupils, (in mainstream and special education), and the concomitant tightening up of the control exerted on schools and teachers, by central government, the DES and LEAs, are providing teachers with much stricter definitions of their role and their duties in performing that role, than has previously been the case.

The augur of payment by results, and teacher assessment, currently on the agenda in the accountability stakes; and the expanding market in the production of curriculum/teaching packages, especially in the field of special educational needs, where the adherence to the objectives/skills analysis approach is almost invariable in commercially available materials and resources, is leading to what some sociologists have referred to as the deskilling of teachers (Apple 1982). The teacher's job is being broken down into discrete parts, over which she is increasingly losing control, as she is being presented with popular packages like Distar and Portage, which strictly define what she is to do. The institutional character of schools, their bureaucratic nature and hierarchical organisation make it easy for these messages about what constitutes good teaching, and the requirements for the practice related to them, to move in and take over. This has been especially so in the education of children with severe learning difficulties, where the teacher's role is already defined so much in terms of the therapeutic ideal for individual children, anyway.

Furthermore, the fact that discussion about what constitutes teaching and the teacher's role in the education of children with severe learning difficulties, only occurs within the narrow confines of the operational model of teaching as planning and implementing individual programmes for individual needs, serves to reinforce these pressures.

No notion of how professionalised teaching, and the treatment relationship between pupil and teacher, play a role in the social construction of mental handicap in the special education system, is recognised or acknowledged in the relevant literature. There is no discussion, hardly ever a hint, that the special skills which teachers of children with severe learning difficulties are advised to acquire and master, might actually overstep the mark as teaching. Despite the fact that Sinha can state baldly, that in psychology,

> ... the scientific enterprise has more to do with the theoretical systematisation and legitimation of socially embedded practices than it does with the unveiling of timeless truths ...

and that:

> We can see quite clearly in the case of a concept like intelligence, how socially determined values underlying current practices become translated into a theoretical construct, which in turn lends scientific legitimacy to the self-same practices (Sinha 1981, p. 403),

there is no suggestion that the psychologically informed 'scientific' pedagogy of teaching children with severe learning difficulties, may be illusory, based on socially determined values rather than scientific certainties. And certainly no idea is put forward that it might have consequences that are destructive and handicapping to the child, or that teaching as it is now conceptualised for these children may <u>not</u> be to do with education.

Parallelling the dominance of the skills analysis paradigm in curriculum development the popularist conception of teaching has a similar monopoly. Although there are indications that some

76

teachers are not altogether happy with the present state of affairs and the emphasis on the imperative teaching strategy (Furneaux 1984; Goddard 1983) there are no articulated alternatives readily available to the mass of teachers.

Within the present situation, the role of the teacher as imposer is easy to take up and easy to disguise under the ideology of special needs and its rhetoric of generosity. The new 'special' skills of the teacher for children with severe learning difficulties, on top of the traditional view of teaching as imparting knowledge, together with the skills analysis curriculum, provide quick, easy answers to teachers' dilemmas about what their role is, what they should teach and how, and just what education and teaching is for these children, inside the classroom. The logic of special needs and special teaching easily justifies consequent practice.

The lack of critical analysis and articulated alternatives to the dominant conception of education and teaching for children with severe learning difficulties, mean that even if teachers disagree with the present definition of their role, they have little opportunity to develop a different role and style of teaching. The hierarchical organisation of schools and the perceived power of the headteacher to enforce policy, may convince teachers that such action is nigh on impossible.

Furthermore, in their day-to-day dealings with children, teachers are faced with problems of expediency and compromise. They have to make snap decisions, and have ready responses. The role of the imposer can at least bring some order to a situation which a teacher may feel otherwise would be uncontrollable and chaotic. Teachers almost naturally fall into the role of telling children what to do, of deciding the most appropriate course of action for both the individual and the group, without consulting them, of laying down boundaries for what children can or can't do in their own classroom. Teachers' basic assumptions about children per se, promote the appropriateness of the imposition of their wills, as adults on them, because the children are in the first place, viewed as immature, inexperienced, ignorant of risks and dangers and unable to know their own needs and interests. When working with those children who find it hard to express their wants and desires to others, at least in forms that teachers will recognise, the inclination to impose learning on the child and inculcate the correct response as the teacher sees it and as societal norms define it, is even greater.

Neither do most teachers have the time in the course of their working day to stand back and reflect on their practice or engage amongst themselves in philosophical debates about what constitutes teaching. To a great extent we all tend to act in certain ways because of what is going on around us. Teachers' attitudes are rooted in the actual practices going on around them and in which they engage themselves. As we have shown, ideas of the dependence and inability of children with severe learning difficulties are embedded in the very way special schools are designed, as well as in the way the organisation is run, in the structure of the school day and content of the educational programme. Teachers are not simply puppets, however, responding to actual practices in a passive and unchallenging way. They are actively engaged in the actions which institutionalise not only the inabilities of their pupils but their own behaviour too. This is because of their responsibilities and duties within the education system, and because of their vigorous defence of their personal and professional identities in the face of all comers - the DES, the Inspectorate, other professionals, other staff in the school, parents, and not least pupils.

The role of imposer protects the teacher, in that appearances look good, efficiency can be demonstrated, and behaviourist techniques are renowned for achieving success in teaching set objectives and the required acceptable behaviour in the child.

The teacher's role as organiser of highly structured individual programmes involving direct teaching in the behaviourist mode, creates 'normal appearances' of children paying attention, and being busy, just as the skills analysis approach to curriculum content provides children with skills which make them look more normal. For us, this is teacher control not teaching in the sense of facilitating learning for education. Controlling children, and 'teaching' them so that they achieve the objectives the teacher has set, does not mean that education is happening. Such a definition of teaching involves rigidity and conformity, and hinges on the medical model of mental handicap. It is not about children sharing knowledge and developing understanding so that they are able to act autonomously and independently. It aids the dominant conception of mentally handicapped people. Complying with the present orthodox view of teaching children with severe learning difficulties makes teachers feel needed. It isn't about the education of children with intellectual impairments.

Brennan (1979) suggests that implementing an objectives curriculum liberates the teacher to work creatively in the classroom, since she doesn't have to think out all the curriculum issues herself. In contrast, we are suggesting that the present emphasis on the teacher as a medium through which the children will acquire skills, creates relations of imposition and dependence in the classroom. In this sense it is handicapping both to the teacher and to the child. It devalues their relationship, and both of them as people, as they become respondents of a system.

We have some sympathy with teachers' feelings of frustration and helplessness, when, for example they are faced with acute behaviour problems, violent outbursts, extreme temper tantrums; a situation when everything in the vicinity is in danger of being smashed up or used as missiles; children who appear to be totally withdrawn and show no overt signs of a desire to participate in anything; children who appear to be so disabled by their impairments that they may be unable to respond to education in any of the ways a teacher might ordinarily expect. Given such situations in the education of children with severe learning difficulties, techniques like 'time-out', and behaviourist teaching strategies which offer such high levels of structure and control that they virtually ensure eliciting the desired response, may appear as 'God-sent gifts', and as the only way of coping with such situations. But when the result is the teacher acting as imposer, controlling the opportunities, decisions and responses for the child without regard for his point of view, his desires and wants, then the teacher-pupil relationship is one of professional and client, helper and helped.

As other writers have been at pains to point out (Skilbeck 1973; Illich 1977; Freire 1970), the form of teaching, style of education and the curriculum plan can make the difference between producing 'acquiescent, docile and socially uninvolved people' and pupils seeing and continuing to see themselves as 'organisers of their own experiences and of their own society' (Skilbeck 1973; p. 34). Williams (1961) asserts that human learning is the most valuable resource we have, and Friere (1970) that apart from enquiry people are not truly human. Education should therefore be about fostering learning and inquiry not limiting it to a banal form of socialisation. Freire (1970) utilises the concepts of education as banking, and education as problem-posing. As banking, education is about teachers depositing knowledge and skills in the pupils. The teacher teaches, the pupils are taught; the teacher decides content and required outcomes, the pupils adapt; the teacher is the subject of the process, while pupils are objects of it:

> The oppressed are regarded as the pathology of the healthy society, which must therefore adjust these ... folk to its own patterns by changing their mentality. These marginals need to be 'integrated', 'incorporated' into the healthy society ... (Freire 1970, p.140).

In contrast, problem-posing education ends the polarisation of pupil-teacher, is about people in their relations with the world, rather than abstracted from it, and is consequently concerned with reality as a process in constant transformation, striving for 'the emergence of consciousness and critical intervention in reality' (Freire 1970, p. 145). It is concerned with creativity in its broadest sense and with the ideas that people matter and people can change things.

These ideas are not irrelevant to people with mental handicaps and to the education of children with severe learning difficulties - because of the consequences for them in provisions and practices that they are subjected to; because of the continuing ideas about how we define mental handicap, people with mental handicaps, and the learning difficulties of children; because of how our attitudes are enshrined and entwined in these things; and because people with mental handicaps are themselves demanding that we change our practice and expectations and offer some of the power to them. Furthermore we have to confront the role of implicit assumptions and taken for granted beliefs, the way these may act on us at an unconscious level to produce unrecognised consequences, and thus the way scores of well-intentioned and caring teachers may fail to realise that their practice serves to dehumanise and erect barriers for those people whom they are trying hard to help.

Chapter Four

BREAKING THE MOULD

Recognition that people with mental handicaps can
speak authoritatively about their needs and can
successfully take on participating roles in the
planning and provision of services, is beginning to
have a direct impact on the organisation of provision and professional practice.

Self advocacy is about people with mental
handicaps speaking for themselves and demanding
their rights and entitlements as fellow human
beings.

In the summer of 1984 there was a self
advocacy conference in London at which people with
mental handicaps spoke for themselves about their
ideas, views and wishes. Garry Bourlet, a past
chairman of the Mencap Metropolitan Self Advocacy
Forum, was one of the contributors. The following
is some of what he had to say:

Setting up a self advocacy group is a great
experience .... Your part is to make it a free
and more normal life ... We are human beings,
not robots. We don't need people to control
our lives. They control us as if we were, but
we can't control them, as they see it in their
way. Self advocacy enables us to make choices
and make our decisions and to enable us to
control the way that lives should be made.
When we need help we ask for it, not to be
told ...

You need to be given time and encouragement.
The more chances to speak you get the easier
it is. It's degrading that people speak for
you, treating you as a kid, but there are
people who haven't been given a chance because
of this (G. Bourlet 1984 quoted in CMH

Newsletter 38, p. 9).

People with mental handicaps have been joining together and speaking up about their wants and needs, and what they think of the services provided for them, for some time in Scandinavia and America. In July 1984 People First of Washington State, USA, organised the first international self advocacy conference for people with mental handicaps, their advisers and supporters. There were 18 delegates from Britain, as well as delegates from as far afield as Australia and New Zealand. Some of the workshop sessions included such topics as 'getting parents to let go'; 'consumers interviewing staff for job vacancies'; 'labelling'; 'how to influence government'; 'doing a self advocacy newsletter'; and 'how to evaluate services you use'. The conference voted to hold the second international conference in 1988 in England (CMH Newsletter 38, 1984).

The roots and growth of self advocacy have been different in different countries and localities. In Sweden in the 1960s, the national authorities took an initial role in recommending that consultative bodies of handicapped people should be established within provisions for them, such as group homes, institutions, sheltered workshops, special schools (Crawley 1983). In the USA many groups developed locally in the 1970s, having bases in friendships and common situations, such as when people were moved out of State institutions into community settings. The development of self advocacy was part of people getting together, socialising, becoming involved in running their own meetings, deciding what they wanted to do, and setting out to do it. Project Two, of Omaha, was one of the first groups of this kind and was formed by ex-residents of the local State institution. They have been very much involved in campaigning for the closure of the same institution. At the same time, State-wide and nationwide conventions have been taking place, initially inspired by professionals impressed by what was happening in Sweden, and later set up and conducted by people with mental handicaps themselves. 'People First International' is now a self advocacy movement run by and for people with mental handicaps, which has chapters (local branches) in many different States and cities in America. It is through this movement that work-shops, State and national conferences are

organised. The 1981 Convention was attended by
2,500 people (Crawley 1983). There are now more
than 70 local or state groups contributing to not
only their own support, as individual groups, but
also to the development of a co-ordinated network
(Williams and Shoultz 1982). The group in Oregon,
who originally adopted the name 'People First',
decided to establish People First International,
and have taken a leading role in the development of
the self advocacy movement both in America and
internationally.

In England in the early 1970s, the Campaign
for Mentally Handicapped People (CMH) organised a
series of three 'Participation' events in which
people with mental handicaps and non-handicapped
people (various professionals and friends)
discussed aspects of the lives of the participants
with mental handicaps, and how they felt. Other
such events have subsequently followed. The
development of self advocacy here in England, has
also been given impetus through the establishment
in Adult Training Centres (ATCs) of trainees'
committees. In 1980 it was found that 22 per cent
of Centres had some form of trainee representation,
and 9 per cent used to have (Crawley 1983). By
1981 at least 17 more committees had been formed
throughout the country. Although Crawley's survey
shows that the commonest type of trainee
representation was in the form of several trainees
regularly meeting with one or two staff members,
rather than having fully fledged 'trainee only'
committees elected by the body of trainees, there
are ATCs in the country where committees have been
formed along these lines. Here self advocacy and
participation of the trainees in the decision
making processes of the centres is really occurring
(e.g. Williams and Shoultz 1982). Where people
with mental handicaps have formed groups of this
kind for themselves (usually with the assistance of
an adviser who is either an independent person from
outside of the centre, or a member of staff), they
have become involved with self advocacy in a
similar way to their American colleagues. For
example, the Student Committee at Avro ATC in Essex
have, among other things, visited and spoken to
trainees at the other centres, have negotiated with
the National Union of Students for union membership
(hence are called students), and participated in
the BBC's 'Let's Go' television programme about
self advocacy (Crawley 1983; Williams and Shoultz
1982). The Pyenest self advocacy group (Pyenest

Centre, Harlow, Essex) campaigned with badges and leaflets distributed around the country, to persuade MENCAP (The Royal Society for Mentally Handicapped Children and Adults) to change their logo - 'Little Stephen' - because they felt he provoked pity and sadness from others towards them, due to his sad, lost and pathetic expression. The group from Pyenest wanted to change other people's ideas about people with mental handicaps and the logo of 'Little Stephen' didn't help their cause.

There are also now some groups which function independently from ATCs or other institutions such as a group in Camden which is consulted by the Social Services regarding facilities and services. In November 1981 what became the Mencap Metropolitan Self Advocacy Forum was formed when ten representatives from ATC trainee committees in the area began to meet on a regular basis, with larger meetings every quarter. This group has now organised several conferences where papers have been presented and views exchanged by and between people with mental handicaps from the locality.

The constitutions drawn up by various trainee committees in ATCs and other more independent self advocacy groups, as well as the contents of reports coming out of proceedings at conference days and conventions over the last few years, all emphasise the same messages and feelings from people with mental handicaps themselves:

> We are individuals; we are human beings; we have the same rights as everyone else; we are important and we have got things to say; we should be listened to; you should listen to us (e.g. Crawley 1983; Williams and Shoultz 1982; CMH Newsletters).

These messages are being reiterated internationally as well. Furthermore, when expressing how they feel about being 'mentally handicapped' and what it means, they consistently draw attention to the negative attitudes of other people who interact with them; how they are not allowed, or are not given the opportunities to do things and live in ways in which other people do; the lack of respect, privacy and choice afforded to them; and the inhumane conditions and treatment meted out to some of their less fortunate peers who do not have self advocacy groups where they can express themselves and gain support, or who still live in particular institutions (e.g. Brandon and Ridley 1983).

People First, of California, have recently compiled a report, for example, called 'Surviving in the system: mental retardation and the retarding environment' (1984), based on a survey of different services and interviews with people with mental handicaps, their families and professionals. Their findings suggest that the traditional system of services for mentally retarded people, its nature and effect, is retarding (CMH Newsletter 39, 1984).

In England the impact of the idea of people with mental handicaps authoritatively speaking for themselves and participating in the planning, organisation and implementation of services can be seen through various initiatives. The growth of ATC trainee committees and groups such as the Mencap Metropolitan Self Advocacy Forum have already been mentioned. Other specific instances include, for example, Calderstones Hospital appointing a person with mental handicap to its clothing and catering committee, the participation workshops held in Clywd as part of the Clywd Plan for services for people with mental handicaps, and the canvassing done of consumers' views by the Erewash Development Group for Mental Handicap Services in Derbyshire, which included people with mental handicaps drawing up a questionnaire, as well as acting as interviewers and being interviewed themselves (CMH Newsletters 37 and 38, 1984).

On the one hand special education for children with severe learning difficulties in England, views itself as enabling the full participation of people with mental handicaps in the communities in which they live, especially in terms of the adults to be, because of the overt emphasis on independence as the major aim and the specialised teaching employed to improve children's repertoires of skills. F.Green, former HMI, has suggested that England is leading the international field in curriculum development for children with severe learning difficulties (National Portage Association Conference 1984).

On the other hand, however, the present orthodoxy's view of education and teaching does not warrant optimism in terms of future adults with mental handicaps being better equipped from the outset to speak up for themselves, to assert their ability (as well as their rights) to make significant decisions about their life circumstances, and directly participate in controlling their own lives. This is because their

education is about teaching discrete skills which
don't usually have anything to do with controlling
one's own life and making decisions, and because
skills are currently taught in a way that
institutionalises dependence. The present trends
in the education of children with severe learning
difficulties fall far short, if they are not
detrimental to the whole idea of people with mental
handicaps speaking for themselves, or being able to
do so after having completed their special
education courses at school. The orthodox view of
children with severe learning difficulties as
recipients of special education, and education as
normalising them, is fundamentally opposed to participation and full and equal rights, on the grounds
of disablity, the need for protection and professional help and control in determining what are in
the children's best interests.

In fact it can be argued that the education
system in England does not acknowledge that people
with mental handicaps have the same basic human
rights as anyone else, and rather that educational
practice contravenes international agreements by
discriminating against children with severe learning difficulties on the grounds of their 'mental
handicap' in a way which has negative consequences.
The United Nations Declaration of the Rights of the
Child, 1959, (Principle 10), the European Convention on Human Rights, 1965, (Article 14) and the
United Nations Declaration of the Rights of
Disabled Persons, 1975, (Article 10), all refer to
the rights of people being secured without discrimination - this includes the right to have
special needs taken into consideration and being
entitled to measures to increase self reliance, and
live life on a par with ordinary peers. Yet as the
Children's Legal Centre point out, 'young people
with mental or physical disabilities are discriminated against - denied access to ordinary institutions and given limited opportunities for education
and training' (Childright 1983, p. 13). Children
with severe learning difficulties are discriminated
against within the education system because of the
segregated nature of their schooling and their lack
of access to ordinary educational provision. The
most recent example of the continuance of a
definite policy of discrimination is in the trend
to provide further education for these young
people, until the age of 19 years, at the
parent's request - not the young person's - not
usuallyin further education facilities but within

the special school which the young person is already attending. Furthermore, Article 3 of the European Convention (1965) and Article 10 of the UN Declaration of the Rights of Disabled Persons (1975) state respectively that, 'No-one shall be subjected to ... inhuman or degrading treatment or punishment' and 'Disabled persons shall be protected against all regulations and all treatment of a ... abusive or degrading nature'. If challenged on the use of certain techniques in educational practice for children with severe learning difficulties such as 'time-out' in time-out rooms, withdrawal of food, use of restraints for purposes other than children's safety, a local education authority may have a hard time in proving that such practices were not '... inhuman or degrading treatment or punishment' or of an 'abusive or degrading nature'.

In part this situation is a reflection of ideas about children's rights, as opposed to people's rights, the differential protection to be afforded to children and differential expectations concerning their capabilities and experience according to maturation. In fact the UN Declarations and the European Convention concerning people's rights do not refer to a lower age limit and are taken to include children. Where children's rights are referred to, it is in terms of guaranteeing protection against, for example, exploitation, and is therefore seen in terms of 'addition to' basic human rights, not instead of. In these cases the age of majority in the country concerned is taken as the legal upper age limit. However, the present situation for children with severe learning difficulties is also a reflection of thinking about the needs of children with disabilities and, in this case, the needs also of people with mental handicaps. As Principle 5 of the UN Declaration of the Rights of the Child (1959) says, 'The child who is physically, mentally or socially handicapped shall be given the special treatment, education and care required by his particular condition'. Present lines of thinking dictate that children with severe learning difficulties require special educational provision.

Special schools for children with severe learning difficulties are often viewed by the professionals and parents concerned as places where the children are accepted and regarded as normal, on their own terms. Frequently, parents still express gratefulness for a place and for specialised help for their child, rather than questioning the kind of help and education given. Teachers are seen as dedicated, wonderfully patient people. Special schools do not, on the whole (although sometimes they do, too), reject these children whereas other schools and other institutions do. Many parents experience their child being rejected and being viewed as abnormal, whereas in the special school he is not so different.

But the aim of special education for children with severe learning difficulties is to change their behaviour and make them more socially acceptable. The acceptance of these children in special education is in terms of what they, the pupils, are - 'mentally handicapped' children - and the consequent allowances which can be made for their behaviour and capabilities. Acceptance is not of who they are in terms of people with rights as they stand. Who they are has come to be defined in terms of what they can do - capabilities and potential. They are defined as children with problems by the very nature at present of the provision of special education. The assumption that children with severe learning difficulties have problems, or are problems in themselves, stems from the concern with what they are and can't do, rather than who they are, and is linked directly to the devalued view of people with mental handicaps within society.

> Even though you say you value me as a person, my experiences tell me that you are unable to distinguish me from my disability. Your society operates as if my disability and the problems it presents are the most important, and perhaps the only thing worth mentioning about me.... Once I ... am seen as a 'problem', it becomes increasingly difficult for you to view me as a real human being. The question of 'what do I as a person need?' becomes 'How do you deal with me, this problem?' Too often your thinking begins to follow this logic:
> ... 'This person is disabled!'
> ... 'His/her disability is a problem!'
> ... 'This problem needs to be fixed!'
> ... 'Special people are needed to fix it!'
> ... 'It can only be fixed in special places!'
> ... 'It needs to go to one of those special places to be fixed!'

'It can only come back, or come out, when 'it' is fixed!'

This scenario is one of the most real and most overwhelming barriers that stands between me and the rest of the world (Pespectives on traditional approaches in Brost et al. 1982, p. 4).

The self advocacy movement amongst people with mental handicaps has highlighted the critical need for education in terms of these people's own views of themselves, their capabilities and their rights, and in terms of professional and public attitudes towards them, the services they are offered, and professional practice. But the education that self advocacy groups participate in, and what they want to see more of, is in terms of people with mental handicaps knowing and understanding:

* that they are human beings and individuals;
* that there is nothing wrong in being different, and all people should be themselves (rather than try to be someone they are not);
* that they have to accept others and their differences if they expect to be accepted themselves;
* that as human beings they have the same rights as everybody else, but that this also involves taking responsibility for their own lives and acting in a responsible way towards others;
* that if they are unhappy with things, feel wronged or unfairly treated etc they can do something about it;
* that doing all these things is exciting and is what living is all about.

Without the participation demanded by rights and responsibilities, they are not living a full life. This is as well as, not instead of, learning to do more activities concerned with daily living. Ray Loomis, the person who founded Project Two, Omaha, USA, said, 'If you think you are handicapped you might as well stay indoors. If you think you are a person, come on out and tell the world' (quoted in Williams and Shoultz 1982, p. 17).

Being able to speak for oneself, and demand one's own entitlements is in part to do with self image, self confidence and identity, but it is also to do with learning the skills of self advocacy on

a very practical day to day basis - how to find out
information, how to contact people who can do something to help you resolve a problem, how to participate in or conduct a meeting - and having basic
knowledge and experience of what rights are, and
the rights and responsibilities individuals can
claim and must abide by. As IDC (Independent Development Council for People with Mental Handicap,
1984) point out, in England there is little opportunity for people with mental handicaps systematically to learn self advocacy skills, and there is a
lack of understandable materials on civil and legal
rights for individuals and groups to refer to.

However, there is another significantly different way in which the self advocacy of people with
mental handicaps has highlighted the critical
nature of education, and this is in the terms of
the fact that, 'Self advocacy means assuming
greater control over your own life - and that must
mean other people exercising less control. This
can be a problem for staff as well as for families'
(IDC 1984, p. 75) - and for planners, administrators, bureaucracies and organisations. In fact it
applies to anyone, or group of people who come into
contact with individuals and groups whom they
assume are 'mentally handicapped'. As is implied by
materials about self advocacy (Crawley 1983; Williams and Shoultz 1982) and suggested by the IDC
(1984), the way to overcome this problem is through
'providing opportunities for non-handicapped people
to learn about self advocacy, and in particular,
what its implications are for them' (IDC 1984, p.75)

There is some contrast between the ideas and
concepts about education mentioned above, and present trends in educational practice and curriculum
development for children with severe learning difficulties within the special education system. This
is because the latter is concerned with the
development of specific skills, and not decision-
making processes, rights and attitudes.

The logical and moral necessity of the current
view of education and mental handicap is to teach
discrete, functional skills where they are lacking
so to better the end product and move it towards
the aim of independence. The logic of this process
appears natural, self evident, commonsensical, and
at the level of appearances, to be in line with the
development of self advocacy in adulthood. But
what is missed out is that ideas about self
advocacy and present ideas about educational
provision and practice in schools involve totally

different starting points, and fundamentally different assumptions about people and about what education is, and is for. One is directly concerned with individuals, self determination and power, while the other is directly concerned with conditions and problems - mental handicap or severe learning difficulties.

What we are talking about are lines of thinking which involve basic assumptions and value judgements underlying what we, as professionals, do with, for and to children with severe learning difficulties and people with mental handicaps. Lines of thinking are not merely expressed in our attitudes towards these children, but also affect what happens and how we treat them. There are direct consequences for the clients of our services (and also for professionals providing services) in terms of the barriers put up which separate them from us, assign particular roles, and make available certain opportunities rather than others, including the power - or lack of it - to affect personal circumstances.

The traditional line of thinking about mental handicap, education and the provision of special education is expressed in the following:

> Your line of thinking prevents you from asking the right questions about me and about other people with disabilities, and our needs. The questions that you ask focus on what is wrong with me and are designed to determine my levels of functioning and the degree of severity of my disability. The results are usually a short perfunctory list of my 'strengths' and long lists of what I <u>cannot</u> do, as well as lists of ... (what is needed) ... to 'fix' me ... When my needs become defined as service types, professionals and places (e.g. 'he needs physical therapy, a behaviour management expert, a group home'), it is easy to lose sight of my more basic human needs that your services were meant to address in the first place. Too often your services are designed and arranged in ways that ignore my current and potential, natural, unpaid supports and in ways that restrict my growth, maintain my dependency and deny me opportunities for community presences and participation (Brost et al. 1982, p. 5).

In contrast, the line of thinking which begins

with the assertion that people with mental handicaps are individuals with rights which must be upheld, puts the individual, rather than his problems, at the forefront of provision and practice within services. Fundamentally different assumptions about the nature and meaning of disability, and the purpose of service provision are involved:

> All people, with or without disabilities, share the same basic needs. As human beings all of us are concerned about having experiences that provide us with (a) autonomy and independence, (b) individuality, (c) love and acceptance through presence and participation within a family and community, (d) continuous growth and learning, (e) community status, (f) security, with respect to finances as well as protection of our legal and human rights. People who have disabilities do not have qualitatively different kinds of needs. Description of disability is relevant only to the extent that the disability condition complicates the fulfilment of the above mentioned needs ... The form of help and the ways in which it is designed and arranged determine whether or not people get their basic human needs met ... Services should be designed and delivered to enhance each person's capacity for growth and to convey the conviction that each person can participate in some valued role in the community. This goal is valid regardless of (a) the type of disability or problems presented, (b) the extent to which the disability complicates service provision, (c) current lack of services required by the person, (d) scores achieved on tests or scales, (e) past involvement with the service system (Brost et al. 1982, pp. 4 - 5).

Qualitatively different perceptions of people with disabilities stem from, and are encouraged by, the emphasis on the individual, or the emphasis on his disability or his problems. Williams and Shoultz (1982) polarise some of the personal perceptions of people with mental handicaps which determine our expectations and behaviour towards them. These are some of their suggestions:

Valuable, serious people who can act responsibly	Trivial foolish people who need to be entertained all the time
Capable of self confidence and courage	Weak, ineffectual
Capable of learning skills of ... co-operating with others and taking decisions	Lacking the skills to be involved
Having important things to say that are worth listening to	Not having any worthwhile views
Capable of acting unselfishly for the benefit of others	Selfish, incapable of understanding the needs of others
Behaviour and skills are a reflection of the expectations of others	Behaviour and skills are a reflection of inherent mental handicap
Having much to give	Presenting many problems
Capable of having a voice of their own	Needing us to speak for them

(Williams and Shoultz 1982, pp. 125-126).

Assumptions which are predominantly about individuals as human beings, rather than about their disabilities, and perceptions which emphasise capabilities and worth instead of problems and difficulties, have direct implications for education. This is not simply at the level of what the curriculum might consist of and what is taught, but also in terms of what education is considered to be about, who does it, how it is transmitted and evaluated. We have presented our view of what is now being held out to teachers as good educational practice with these children in terms of what should be taught, why and how. The latter doesn't tally with our ideas of what education could be, or should be about. Present trends in the special education of children with severe learning difficulties do not seem to be capable of coping with the idea of these children, and people with mental handicaps, having the same rights as others, and being able and of right being given the space and opportunities to speak for themselves. Crawley notes that: 'choice and determination of one's actions are essential to human dignity' and 'self advocacy skills are needed to some degree almost every day. We protect ourselves from discrimination and exploitation by the knowledge of our rights, and the confidence to act assertively if they are infringed ... To be effective, the right of self determination must be a philosophy underlying the whole of ... life' (Crawley 1983, p. 1). School life for children with severe learning difficulties, seems rather to ignore these sentiments.

THE CONNECTIONS BETWEEN IDEAS ABOUT PEOPLE AND IDEAS ABOUT EDUCATION

When the rights of individuals and people collectively are held up as important, ideas about freedom, the acknowledgement of rights and non-discriminatory practices and provisions are implied. The concept of education suggested within such a framework is that of a broad process concerned with individual growth, power and responsibility, linked to possibilities for self determination and autonomy for people both as individuals and as members of groups. Education would be an on-going process which people actively participate in for its own sake at the time (rather than specifically for the utilitarian ends it might eventually lead to), because it would directly involve the development of individuals' ideas, capabilities and power to assert them.

Such ideas about what education is or should be about are by no means new. That education is concerned with the moral development of the individual, emotions, personality and character, rather than simply intellectual growth and academic achievement, has been asserted by probably all serious educational theorists since Plato. Similarly, those held as great educational thinkers of our time, e.g. Froebel, Rousseau, Montessori, Piaget, Dewey, have placed emphasis on the active participation of learners in their learning and consequently self motivation; the importance of the individual as a unique and whole human being who needs to be treated as such; and the process of education as being a worthwhile activity for its own sake, rather than in terms of its end products. More recently, sentiments such

as these have been central to the so-called
'progressive' education movement, and to 'child
centred' education. As Blenkin and Kelly point
out, to conceive of education in this way is not to
ignore individual career needs or indeed the
acquisition of basic skills and functional
capacities to live and work in society as
independently as possible in the future; rather it
is to claim that, 'such needs should not be allowed
to dominate ... educational planning' (Blenkin and
Kelly 1983, p. 312).

As implied above, ideas about education as a
continuous process of individual growth, involving
self motivation, active participation and as a
worthwhile activity in itself, are underlaid by
certain fundamental beliefs or views about people,
their capacities for learning and potential
development; about how people learn most effectively and what is important in life; what it is important to learn and be able to do. These beliefs are
concerned with the status of all people as valuable
human beings whatever their level of functioning,
or position of power and prestige. All people are
unique and have abilities in some areas or situations and inabilities in others. Human beings are
fundamentally of a social nature and will behave in
certain ways and do certain things because their
behaviour is purposeful to them. Experience is the
basis of learning, and the environment and interaction with other people is crucial to an
individual's development. Participation, co-
operation and negotiation are significant processes
in a growing capacity for self determination and,
conversely, domination is harmful to that capacity.
Different views and different abilities are
valuable and important and not in themselves
reasons for discrimination.

Most, if not all, of the above ideas and
beliefs about people and about education are not
simply implicit (or explicit) in the work of
renowned educationalists, they are also
continuously invoked by present educational
ideology, government reports such as the Warnock
Report (1978) providing prime examples. However,
the contradiction is, as Wilson and Cowell note in
talking about teachers and education in general,
that:

> In fact we would probably all admit that
> learning to make friends (very different from
> merely 'mixing well'), to love people, to

enjoy the arts, to like some kind of work for its own sake (very different from accepting social criteria of employability) and similar achievements are much more worth learning than most of the stuff we put on timetables and in the curriculum. Thus our actual (and surely rational) beliefs about what is worth learning seem at odds with what we teach (Wilson and Cowell 1984, p. 34).

Although liberal and human concerns are frequently paid lip service to, especially in educational circles, when it comes down to practice other things come first or get in the way, and in any case education and schooling are not the same thing. There are other things which impose on schooling, other concerns which have to be taken into consideration. Specifically, these other things have to do along with pressures of time, numbers and resources, with the role of schooling, rather than the broad concept of education. Schooling is particularly concerned with the intellectual development of children and preparing them for adult life in terms of fitting into society and being contributing members. The rhetoric of educational policy maintains that personal growth and development and preparation for adulthood are 'by no means incompatible' (Warnock 1978, 1:4) and that rather the two go hand in hand, whereas others acknowledge that conflicts of interest can be involved and that, 'we must recognise ... that the implication of a view of education as necessarily concerned with the development of the individual must be squarely faced. It cannot be left to happen by chance as a by-product of a largely vocational form of training' (Blenkin and Kelly, 1983, p. 311). In practice what happens is succinctly summed up by Wilson and Cowell:

We may point to the practical importance of achievement and social competence, whatever our higher ideals might be. We may suggest that, to the child at least, such goals as physical achievement and having a job will - whatever our own values - count for more than anything else (Wilson and Cowell 1984, p. 33).

The difficulty is that the two concerns of individual growth and the development of social competence as preparation for adulthood, involve different beliefs, different value judgements and different assumptions about people and about what it is important to learn, to be able to do and to have, which can lead to very different forms of practice. When the emphasis is laid upon social competence and being able to fit into society as it is, and contribute to it in terms of self support and work (as is the case in the present orthodox view of the education of children with severe learning difficulties), ideas concerned with a broad and liberal view of education, and with the rights of individuals as human beings, the quality of human relationships and the power of individuals and groups to determine their own lives, easily become irrelevant, merely ideals, as far as the daily life of classrooms goes. In reality the assumptions underlying practice in schools have much more to do with what is held to be important to live and to get on within our present society, e.g. competence in looking after one's own require-ments, social acceptability, intelligence, good looks, status, money, individual effort and in-dividual success. Of course, along with these values goes the way of responding to individuals with disabilities, which affect their standing according to such values, as problems first and people second.

In one sense these issues have been clouded over by the overtness and vociferousness of calls for accountability, for more detailed and more accurate records and measures of performance and achievement (of teachers as well as pupils), for education to be relevant to the 'needs' of pupils, for schooling to be more directly linked to the requirements of working life and the needs of in-dustry and employers, and by the 'back to basics' movement. In another sense, the demands being made of teachers and schools offer compelling reasons for confronting these issues and for individual teachers, at least, to decide what they consider education to be about, what it is for, and what part they play. Instead of residing in the com-fortable and taken for granted view of learning in school as education and not indoctrination, the present framework of debate is highlighting the role of schooling in socialisation, and for those who care to reflect on their teaching and the pressures being exerted for them to teach certain things in certain ways, the differences and con-nections between education, indoctrination and training are being heightened.

Neither are the differences and connections between education and indoctrination, traditional teaching and progressive education that simple or straightforward. Some have suggested that so called child-centred and progressive education represents traditional teaching in a generous guise, and that the same value judgements and expectations of pupils, in terms of ability, appearance and behaviour, still act as crucially important factors in their educational progress, or lack of it, and the opportunities afforded to them (e.g. Sharp and Green 1975). 'Progressive' education too has apparently earned itself a dubious notoriety, and has been connected to the indoctrination of left-wing ideas (e.g. the Black Papers of the 1960s and early 1970s, and the furore of the William Tyndale affair). Even the present emphasis on standards, a return to traditional values, assessing and responding to individual needs, and the importance placed on the back to basics movement, has its contradictions in our consumer-oriented society, with the rapid growth of technological advance. Blenkin and Kelly (1983) ask, for example, what now constitutes the needs of society, the vocational interest of the individual, or basic skills? A further area of controversy lies in the beginnings of recognition of firstly parents and secondly pupils as consumers of education, who therefore are seen as having some right to a say in what that education consists of, not simply in terms of it being relevant to children's needs, wants and requirements, but also in their participation in the organisation and running of schools.

Most of these ideas have never been applied to the education of children with severe learning difficulties as it has developed as part of the special education system since 1970. The issues raised have not been confronted in debate within professional circles about what education for these children might be like. For example, progressive education, as it has developed in infant and junior schools, has not, on the whole, been viewed as relevant to 'mentally handicapped' children, both because of the children's special educational needs, and thus their inability in situations that are not formally structured. This is despite the fact that other practices, materials and activities very much associated with infant education have been incorporated wholesale, such as emphasis on and techniques of teaching pre-number and pre-reading skills. Although there are a few open plan special schools, and although special education claims to respond to individual needs and be child-centred because of the emphasis on individual programme planning, the questions of what role pupil participation should play in the organisation and running of special schools catering for children with severe learning difficulties, and what might constitute indoctrination, education or training in their education have not been debated, as if they are not relevant. Schools councils, for example, and children with severe learning difficulties running their own, seem at the moment not simply ideals, but misplaced visions and misguided, romantic notions about their capacities as children with severe handicaps and inherent incapabilities.

The issues raised so far in the book, in the terms of what present trends in the education of children with severe learning difficulties imply, and how people with mental handicaps are breaking down traditional views of their inabilities and incompetence: the assumptions and value judgements embedded in practice and connections between ideas about education and ideas about people, have direct implications for us as educators of children with severe learning difficulties. We need to begin to examine our practice critically and raise alternatives to dominant trends. Teachers must address themselves to the questions of:

* what mental handicap or severe learning difficulty means in terms of education;
* what education means in relation to mental handicap;
* what assumptions mental handicap, severe learning difficulty and education are based on;
* what value judgements they involve about people;
* what the consequences might be for all participants - teachers and pupils alike;
* what education should be for;
* what it should, could or might consist of;
* how it could, should occur;
* and WHY in relation to all these questions.

In the light of all the points and questions raised, we suggest that the following become major issues for both teachers and pupils, as people and participants, in the education of children with severe learning difficulties. These issues have to be faced, rather than ducked or ignored as presently seems the case, if there is to be a

fuller understanding of the activities that we are
concerned with as educators, and what might be
involved in constructively changing the way we
work. The issues to be addressed have been
polarised for effect and simplicity, but if
statements on the left-hand side are accepted as
being more to do with the concept of education,
then we are talking about education for children
with severe learning difficulties being about
ameliorating handicapping conditions and breaking
down the barriers that prevent these children and
people with mental handicaps being participating
and self determining people with the power required
to make their wishes known and defend their rights.
What is involved is the power to challenge for
themselves traditional views of them as unable and
irresponsible and second class citizens.

VERSUS

Education as a process	Education as product centred; a means to an end
Underlying assumptions, values and beliefs made explicit and hence open to debate and critical evaluation	Underlying assumptions, values and beliefs implicit, remaining unquestioned
Acknowledging that all people have the same basic rights as human beings. All children have the same rights	The rights of people with mental handicap are necessarily limited because of their mental handicap. Children do not have the same rights as adults. Children with severe learning difficulties and people with mental handicaps never grow up, they are forever child-like
All people are valuable human beings and have abilities and inabilities. People should not be devalued or discriminated against because of their inabilities	Children and adults who have severe learning difficulties are less valuable people

VERSUS

Education is about inter-action between people, and with the environment	Education is about teachers teaching, and pupils learning
Children and adults as active participants in the learning process which is collaborative, co-operative and about sharing	Teachers imposing what is to be in the learned, children as recipients of education
Education being concerned with learning to value oneself and others for WHO they are, and acknowledging that everyone has something to contribute	Education sorting and grading children and adults in relation to their performance, inabilities and behaviour, and assigning worth accordingly
The intrinsic value of the learning process and the importance of self motivation and respect for individual choices, and desires	Teaching centred around the use of extrinsic motivation and the teacher imposing what she knows best
The needs and interests of individuals acknowledged and respected	The interests and needs of others, and the establishment over-ruling those of individuals
Education about fostering, encouraging and facilitating trust, autonomy and initiative, involving the development of responsible and self determining people	Schooling as about control and conformity. Children lacking responsibility and teachers as agents within the system. Children depend upon teachers for their education, and teachers are dependent upon the system for what they teach and how they teach, and for their status and position as imparters of knowledge

It is teachers who are responsible for their own
practice; it is they who must confront the issues
involved if they are to be more fully aware of the
consequences of their own practices; and it is they
who are in a position to change basic elements of
their own practice, such as the personal relationships imposed by styles of teaching and the value
judgements implied by actions which relate to fundamental assumptions about children and people,
mental handicap and values in society, as well as
to their own view of their role and job.

PROCESSES OF LEARNING AND PRINCIPLES OF ORGANISATION

To emphasise education for children with
severe learning difficulties as a process where the
rights of individuals are respected and people are
valued for who they are and their contributions
accepted as worthwhile whatever they might be, does
not mean that education doesn't or shouldn't
include the skills presently specified by the
skills analysis approach, or that structure is not
important. What is crucial is how things are
taught and in what form, and therefore what kind of
structure is employed. Neither does it entail the
denial of conflict between people's needs and
interests, or between the needs of individuals and
those of the school as an institution.

Rather it is about recognising those
conflicts, and developing co-operative,
collaborative and negotiated ways of working,
instead of allowing consciously or by default, the
domination of certain needs or requirements over
others.

We are not concerned here to promote or in any
way explain or describe a complete educational
programme for children with severe learning
difficulties, as is currently the trend in
producing curriculum packages and books given over
to 'tips for teachers'. It seems important to
spell this out because so often in reading a book
like this, which attempts to question present
practice, readers, particularly teachers, seem to
expect and want the authors to tell them what to do
instead. But set answers inevitably involve
fitting children into schemes, not responding to
individuals. Furthermore, such an enterprise is
dehumanising and devaluing to teachers themselves
because it puts them in subservient positions of
'receiving wisdom', not thinking about their own
situations and the implications of different views

or theories, and the inter-relating factors involved which are unique to different individuals, different settings, backgrounds, talents, difficulties and so on. It would therefore be contradictory to the idea of education as a process (rather than a means to a specified end) to suggest that a particular set of activities, materials, skills to be learned and teaching techniques made up such a process oriented approach. We could describe some of our own experiences in trying to implement ideas connected to this approach and in trying to implement an adherence to individual rights in practice, rather than simply holding this as an idealistic notion. However, to do justice to such an enterprise would require another volume at least, and still leaves open the possibilty of others taking things which we have found to work well in particular situations and groups, and incorporating them wholesale into their own practice and into situations and groups which are quite different. It isn't the answers that are crucial in terms of solutions to difficulties, activities to promote, materials to use; it is the questions posed and the principles used to examine and raise alternative courses of action.

The issues identified previously as needing to be faced in providing education for children with severe learning difficulties, suggest a basic dichotomy between a process oriented approach and an instrumental approach. The present trends in curriculum planning and teaching - to translate aims into objectives and tasks to be mastered - are appropriate to the instrumental approach. The process oriented approach demands rather that assumptions, values and beliefs be made explicit, and be translated into principles for action. This involves a continuous reciprocal relationship between theory and practice and a conscious and never ending questioning of what is happening in and around the situations and relationships in which teachers and children participate. Teachers have to accept their own responsibility for their own practice, examining, reflecting upon, modifying and redesigning the ways they work, in critical analysis and evaluation with colleagues and children. What we are concerned to do here is provide starting points and avenues for exploration which show:- the significance of lines of thinking; that there can be constructive and practical alternatives to present trends in practice; and that education, mental handicap and severe learning difficulty are not given, but are constructed in our ways of working, perceiving and responding to individuals.

Learning, associated with an emphasis upon education as a process and acknowledging the rights and value of all individuals, is an interactive experience involving the sharing of knowledge and understanding so that children can use knowledge autonomously. Dearden (1968 quoted in McConkey 1981) differentiates between (1) superficial knowledge, the 'knowing of' level which is the acquisition of facts and skills at second hand, and which are believed and accepted solely on the authority of another person; and (2) personal knowledge which is understanding. Learning in terms of education is about the development and growth of understanding, not just the acquisition of knowledge at the 'knowing of' level. The acquisition of skills is therefore far more than the mastery of tasks which comprise aspects of what is necessary to perform - rather than understand - the skill. A process oriented approach involves a continuing series of activities and experiences which always have direct and personal purpose for the individuals who are participating. Learning and education would therefore be of intrinsic value to the individual and involve a major element of self direction. Providing for learning, within education as a process, is about providing opportunities for personal and social growth and development of people as unique individuals, as social human beings and as members of groups. Strategies, abilities and capacities are encouraged, promoted and developed, enhancing self actualisation, intrapersonal and interpersonal relationships. This creates the ability for children and teachers to relate to increasingly complex situations and environments, following the directions in which the participants themselves wish to go. The starting point is what people can do, enhancing and developing that, rather than finding out what they can't do and setting out to teach it.

Once it has been accepted that children with severe learning difficulties are valuable human beings with the same rights as everyone else, any overall purpose of education, aside from individual's own purposes in specific actions and activities, must logically take this assertion into account. It could be considered therefore that in wanting to provide education (rather than training or indoctrination), development in the following dimensions is involved:-

(1)   awareness of the self as a unique and important individual gaining increasing levels of self actualisation, self realisation and self determination;
(2)   expansion of individuals' capacities to cope with and gain from ever enlarging environments involving an increasing range of opportunities and augmentation from the self to the group;
(3)   social awareness and group membership with respect for and understanding of the rights of others and an acceptance of others' importance and value, on a par with one's own.
      A significant demand of educators would be to acknowledge that all behaviour engaged in by people - adults and children - is purposeful and meaningful to them. People have different interpretations of what is going on, of objects, events, situations, kinds and levels of interaction, just as they have personal likes and dislikes. There are certain ways of perceiving what is going on, which adults in particular share, which allow us all to continue our lives according to commonsense assumptions and beliefs. For example, if you wait at the bus stop, the bus will come sooner or later; if you walk into the middle of the road you stand a relatively good chance of getting knocked down. Children, whatever their level of functioning have reasons for doing or not doing things, but obviously they do not completely share the commonsense assumptions that are taken for granted in adulthood. These have to be acquired, learned, taken in. If behaviour is seen as purposeful, then it has to be accepted as (in this case) a child's way of coping with and responding to his world, according to his perceptions of it, and his avenues for expressing those perceptions. Children with severe learning difficulties may initially have and may develop very particularistic perceptions of what is going on around them, not least because of their intellectual impairments. They may view things in ways which are very difficult for us, as adults, to imagine because of the different experiences being involved. As professionals, we do not know what it must be like to have an intellectual impairment. We seem to find it difficult enough to remember and take into consideration what it is like to view things from and through the less experienced (in in terms of time) eyes of children, who share

a basic grasp of our common language, let alone to
envisage things from the points of view of those
with whom we have great difficulties communicating
and relating. But to be involved in a process and
rights oriented approach to education demands the
striving for this level of understanding. We have
to work towards an appreciation of links between
thinking and acting, perceiving and responding, in
the context of the material practices around ourselves. This is not simply central to the
teachers' interaction with children in terms of
respect for and acceptance of them as valuable
human beings - because of the necessity to accept a
child's behaviour as an investment of himself in
action of some kind which is of value to him and
must not be ignored or deprecated if he is to be
accepted as a fellow human being with important
things to say. It is also central to the inter-
relations of theory and practice, and to attempts
to make explicit assumptions underlying practice,
to understanding consequences or possible consequences of practices and to evaluating the pre-
suppositions and concepts being used - or abused.

A process oriented approach to education,
acknowledging the rights and value of all
individuals, therefore involves a total rejection
of the simplistic behaviourism preached within the
orthodox approach to teaching children with severe
learning difficulties (as embodied for example in
EDY; Kiernan 1981; Crawford 1980). This is
predominantly because the simplicity of
presentation is a misleading representation of the
complexity and uniqueness of individual reponses,
and because it thereby leads practitioners to
ignore the value of individuals' behaviour to
themselves and to employ methodology without a
thorough appreciation of what is involved.
Behaviour modification and behaviouristic methods
have made available to teachers, on a supposedly
scientific footing, powerful techniques for
changing behaviour which as we have shown are
utilised within a framework where the fundamental
assumptions are those of the professional-client
relationship, involving imposition, dehumanisation
and discrimination. This is because of the power
differentials embodied in the assumptions and
practices. We are not suggesting that there is
nothing of use at all within the behaviourist
approach and the principles of learning that have
been highlighted. We would not deny, for example,
the utility of analysing tasks in terms of what has

to be done to complete a specific task, or chaining and shaping as useful techniques in teaching, nor indeed the importance of positive reinforcement. Rather we see the necessity for a thorough examination of the assumptions being made whenever such techniques are used, whether formally or informally, so that teachers, as professionals responsible for their own practice, can make principled decisions about that practice. This is instead of doing something in a particular way 'because it works', and therefore unappreciative of the unintended consequences of their actions, let alone the value judgements they are implicitly employing which may involve them in dehumanising practices without their conscious knowledge and despite their contrary efforts and intentions.

A process oriented approach which holds that self determination and intrinsic motivation are important elements in learning in an educative manner would reject those behaviourist techniques which deal solely with extrinsic control mechanisms, such as the application of rewards essentially to get a child to do something - e.g. a plate of chopped up chocolate buttons on the table, the teacher says, 'Look at me' or 'Sweetie', pops a piece of chocolate into the child's mouth when he responds; or to stop a child from doing something, such as the use of time-out. Instead, self control would be seen as something that has to be built upon from the very beginning rather than shaped after the particular product of behaviour has supposedly been mastered according to the teacher's external criteria. This would not mean, for example, that we would let a child having a very aggressive outburst of behaviour continue to destroy what was around him (especially if it wasn't his) or hurt those near him. To start with, care would be taken to avoid such a situation occurring in the first place. If however it did occur, then either the child himself would be led to a safe place away from the other children and things if he was so willing, or else the people and things around him would be quickly got out of the way. Unless a child specifically wanted to be on his own, the teacher would stay with him (at whatever distance was appropriate) and strive to find ways of using the situation positively for the child to understand what was happening and to learn mechanisms of self control through exploring other less destructive outlets for anger, frustration, anxiety or fear. Such a way of dealing with behaviour in the first place recognises its value to the individual concerned and therefore that in his eyes it was an appropriate action to take and, secondly, involves respect for and encouragement of self determination, self control and responsibility for one's own actions from the very outset. A technique such as 'time-out' ignores these elements, except when it is done under a contract basis where the child voluntarily times himself out, understanding what is involved in the situation and why. It is not sufficient to argue that the latter behaviour is that which is learned through being timed-out by someone else, because as we said at the beginning of this section, it is HOW things happen and the form in which they happen which are crucial - not the end results.

No doubt, to many teachers with large groups of demanding children, some of the above sounds hopelessly idealistic and totally impractical. But it isn't. It may be difficult,but then many worthwhile activities are, especially when they involve working out and implementing principles which confront us with our own weaknesses and failures, or bring us into conflict with traditional and popularly established ways of doing things which present formidable opposition.

When education is seen as an interactive process, the social, personal and active elements of learning come to the forefront. The basic mediums through which education occurs for the child and the teacher alike can then be seen as:

(1)　interaction, communication and the development of relationships; and
(2)　the sharing and acquisition of knowledge and understanding.

If you look at people with mental handicaps from the point of view of them having the same rights as all other people, and whose behaviour is relevant, then viewing the mediums of teaching and learning as the important elements of the education process has very practical implications. What is involved is providing an environment in which individuals can express themselves in the way they want. They can then give something of themselves, their understanding, motivation and ways they are presently being self determining, which can be worked with.

This is not a demand for teachers to be trained in totally different techniques. The crux is examining one's own assumptions and beliefs and how these relate to actions. Once it has been accepted that children with severe learning difficulties are individuals with the same basic rights as other people, and therefore the same right to participate in situations in which they are involved, in a self determining manner, other things follow, most notably finding ways of allowing this to happen and being able to recognise when it does - how for example even the most profoundly disabled pupil is an interactive, communicating and self determining person who, given the chance, is quite capable of developing further his own knowledge and understanding. Rather than adhering to the role of expert and implementer of an educational programme designed to achieve end products, the teacher is in the position of sharing her knowledge and understanding and utilising her skills so that the children can participate and develop their own understanding.

Unless the primary element in the professional's value system is the worth of the individual and respect for him as he is, she is not apt to find herself really caring or wanting to understand the individual and his needs, wants and desires. To say that you value individuals for who they are is a lot easier than abiding by the principle in practice. There is nothing 'natural' about its occurrence even when professionals profess to the particular philosophical stance involved. Rather it involves hard work and continual questioning and evaluation from others, points of view, as well as one's own.

In general, and within the education system, people's rights relate to how they are dealt with by others in physical, emotional and social contexts, access to ways of life and services and therefore to discrimination. In terms of what is relevant to education in schools (and leaving aside the question of integration), children's rights can be related to the respect due to them as people and the provision of security, trusting and loving relationships and friendships; the right to seek happiness and contentment; the right to self determination - choice, freedom, decision making and responsibility; and the right to take risks, make mistakes and accept the consequences of their own behaviour (For materials about rights refer to Williams and Shoultz 1982; Crawley 1983).

Meeting rights involves fulfilling needs. As far as the teacher is concerned, her interactive relationship with the children is the main arena in which needs have to be respected and fulfilled, and rights acknowledged. Stevens (1976), for example, suggests that in terms of providing education, 'severely mentally handicapped' children need to be considered firstly as children, rather than the prime concern being their disabilities. She points to the following needs in this regard:

1. To be considered as children capable of growth ...;
2. To have freedom of choice for natural movement and activities in a specially structured environment;
3. To receive continued praise and approval from teachers and others...; from staff seeing behaviour in terms of communication which needs to be interpreted if it is to be understood and gain positive adult response;
4. To have opportunities for play that is understood by the teacher;
5. To have an immediate purposeful response to natural interests and to language;
6. To have a special kind of teacher;
7. To have a varied and stimulating programme of ... activities;
8. To have planned, systematic and sustained individual teaching by the same teacher ... ;
9. To be in an educational climate where all the adults concerned work together for the benefit of the children ... (Stevens 1976, p. 29).

Sensitivity to needs and rights involves re-cognising and developing trust, autonomy and ini-tiative. By trust, we mean to have confidence in oneself and others; to feel safe to act; to feel one has something to give and receive; to be able to predict what will happen in familiar contexts; to have common assumptions with other people about the constancy of events; and therefore to know that any behaviour will be interpreted as communicative and that whatever the behaviour, trust will remain secure within the relationship. By autonomy, we mean the power to determine one's own actions and behaviours and to make one's own decisions in con-trast to other people determining the opportuni-ties, limitations and outcomes. By initiative, we mean the power to begin things for oneself, to have the confidence to take chances, to be able to make decisions for oneself which involve taking risks.

Trust, autonomy and initiative are attributes involved in relationships as inter-related processes of development. In order to allow for and positively encourage trust, autonomy and initiative, certain things are demanded of the relationships between teacher and children and the teachers view of her role. Firstly, equality is demanded in relations. This necessarily involves a dramatic change in the orthodox social relations of teaching which embody massive power differentials, particularly in terms of children with severe learning difficulties. Instead of the dichotomy between teacher-pupil, expert-novice, helper-helped, transmitter-receiver, the teacher must regard herself as a partner of the children in her relations with them and therefore as a learner alongside them. This is not to deny that the teacher is more experienced or skilful than the children, although it would be more conducive for her to regard herself as having different experiences and different skills. It indicates her role as a facilitator, not an imposer. This role of facilitator, in terms of education and learning is about rendering it easy for children to be trusting of themselves and others, to act autonomously and take the initiative within the social context of the group, the classroom and the school. The role demands that teachers demonstrate in their actions adherence to the fundamental assumptions that children with severe learning difficulties are valuable in their own right, have valid contributions to make which are worth taking note of, and have their own wishes and views which should be respected.

The role of facilitator further means accepting the responsibility of arbiter and guide between individual and the group at least initially. The teacher has to have regard to the group context as an arena in which trust, autonomy and initiative can become attributes of individuals' relationships within the group, and to the group as a collective; and also how the group itself can develop a feeling of collectivity, identity and support for members having regard to decision making by the group and self advocacy.

Acceptance is the basic requirement of an enabling environment and therefore the basic strategy available to the teacher in creating one. Acceptance of children, as they are, with what they

do as important and to be respected, is essential
to providing opportunities for, and the development
of, trust, autonomy and initiative. This means,
for example, not discussing a child with other
adults as if he wasn't there when he is; not being
condescending or cynical in communicating in any
way - gesture, body movement, eye contact as well
as verbal language - but rather showing courtesy;
taking the things children say and do seriously;
not punishing children when their behaviour is
predominantly communicative - either physically or
by ridiculing them in front of others, or by withdrawal of privileges such as attention, freedom of
movement and expression; not degrading or regarding
as valueless, useless or aimless, behaviour such as
rocking, twiddling, flapping because it is what the
child does and therefore has meaning for him. Anything a child does however minute, obsessive or
irrelevant (in adult eyes) provides a starting
point in a relationship and a way of beginning to
come to terms with and strive to understand the
child's world from his point of view. Starting
with what the child does acknowledges that:

> The primary root of all educative activity is
> in the instinctive, impulsive attitudes and
> activities of the child, and not in the pre-
> sentation and application of external material
> ... and ... accordingly numberless spontaneous
> activities of children ... are capable of
> educational use, nay, they are the foundation
> stones of educational method (Dewey 1900
> quoted in Blenkin and Kelly 1983, p.258).

It follows that the teacher's sensitivity will
be crucial to her being able to get some idea of
the meaning to the children themselves of actions,
objects or events and to then being able to use
these constructively. There are a number of ways a
teacher can help herself in this regard.

1.   Practise and develop observational skills,
watch children closely in different settings and
observe what happens, how and in what way.
2.   Ensure that the environment in which the
children act is safe and secure so that the
likelihood of having to intervene to guard against
danger, or deal with disruptive or violent
behaviour in a non-facilitative way is minimised.
For example, the room can be organised so that
children have places they can feel are their own,

children have places they can feel are their own, or where they can retreat to safety and/or isolation if they wish; where they can take out their feelings on inanimate objects without hurting or disrupting someone else like in a screened off area of soft furnishings, cushions or a quiet room.
3. Constantly employ a questioning approach to your own actions/responses and activities which you instigate with regard to their relevance to the children; to the observations you make and to whether your organisation is such to allow facilitation, and thus avoid confrontation when that would be destructive.
4. Allow time to observe and question, and see these as of value instead of feeling that you and the children have to be 'busy' and occupied in any traditional sense of the word for education to occur and for the teacher to be in control (e.g. Stevens 1976).
5. View assessment in terms of getting to know children intimately and have some grasp of their point of view, rather than seeing it as being predominantly concerned with their deficits and levels of functioning (e,g. Brost et al. 1982).
6. Develop ways of recording and planning which involve firstly making clear your own assumptions and value judgements and apply objectives to your own behaviour, rather than to tasks the children are to achieve (refer 'expressive' objectives in Stenhouse 1975; Golby et al. 1975) and, secondly, continuous observation of the consequences.
7. Practise and develop skills of interacting and communicating and become aware of facets of these in others.

The kinds of processes important in an enabling environment - interaction, communication, participation, negotiation, collaboration, co-operation and responsibility, - further help to identify kinds of activities, content and teaching strategies which would facilitate their development and enhancement. For example, 'learning about ourselves as people, our feelings, our rights' could be a constant theme (refer for example to some of the materials in Williams and Shoultz 1982; Crawley 1983; Brost et al. 1982). The number and types of activities that can be done by people together, or for each other, in which things of relevance to themselves can be expressed, are endless (It should be noted that these include all so-called basic skills for living, but that privacy is a need should also be remembered).

There are also innumerable ways of encouraging decision making skills both for individuals and within the group as a whole, going from offering simple choices through to holding meetings that involve spokespeople, agendas, and voting. The children's ability to participate successfully is not dependent so much upon their own abilities and inabilities as on (1) the teacher's ability to structure the environment in such a way that success is ensured and any disability which could act as a barrier to participation is circumvented; and (2) on the teacher's sensitivity to the ways in which children with severe learning difficulties express themselves, and what self determination means in their terms.

Illustrative examples at this point might help people who have read so far to grasp the significance of processes and rights for their own practice, in the context of the children they know. On the other hand, such an exercise could be confusing and present a misleading picture. This is because examples would be out of context and could hardly begin to cover the variety of possibilities involved. We are leaving it up to readers themselves to engage in the process of observation, and critical analysis and evaluation of their own behaviour in the context of looking at what their children do and what interaction occurs in teaching. In trying to understand the meaning of human rights in the day-to-day occurrences in the classroom, and in trying to see what ways children are self determining here and now, a teacher will find her own way forward if she so desires, which will be applicable to those particular circumstances and that set of possibilities.

However, there is one example that is illustrative of the issues discussed throughout this chapter and how they relate to our responsibility as educators, which may serve to focus attention on the connections between processes, rights and conditions that are handicapping:

> ... a child in my class, Clare, comes in: she's tearing at her hair, jerking, she's like a thing possessed, she won't smile at you, she can't concentrate on anything. So what do I do? I put her in a warm bath. I use soap bubbles, pour water down her back, work for her relaxation. My job is to ameliorate this

115

uptight little person's condition and if I succeed - is that education? In my view it is her education because it is amelioration of her handicapping condition and in the process an enhancement of her present life experience ... (Serpell-Morris 1982, pp. 177-178).

Within the context of teachers' own interactive experience with the children they are responsible for educating, they do have some powers of control. They can use it to try and plug up the gaps in the children's functioning or they can help the children to use their own minds and enhance who they are at that given moment in time. To choose the latter course is not unrealistic or unfair to the children because of the kinds of environment they may find themselves in at the end of schooling where 'self determination' may not be on the agenda. Rather it is doing something about rights and handicapping conditions now and accepting personal responsibility for such matters at least in those spheres of life in which teachers personally act. It also creates the possibility of children and young people with severe learning difficulties challenging for themselves concepts about mental handicap, and being in positions to negotiate more from future environments. Education might then be more concerned with who in fact people are than with value-laden assumptions about what they should become.

Chapter Five

A NEW DEAL?

An aura of progressiveness and confidence that
children with severe learning difficulties are
being helped to reach their full potential is
created and maintained by espousing normalisation,
individual programme planning, prescriptive
teaching, social education and community participation in policy statements and short and long term
plans for action.
However, the assumption that mentally
handicapped people are fundamentally different to
ordinary people remains in both public and
professional circles.

Historically, mentally retarded persons have
borne a heavy burden of stigma; society, at
times, has perceived them as less than human.
This is not an inevitable response but
attitudes are slow to change; and despite
progressive trends in our society, retarded
persons are still seen as deviants and their
social identities are generally discounted
(Bercovici 1983 p.7).

Indeed we have argued that what have been
welcomed as 'progressive trends' in education - the
development of the core curriculum, precision
teaching, the 1981 Education Act - can have
anything but progressive consequences for children
with severe learning difficulties. This is because
of how these trends have been put into practice and
because underlying assumptions and value judgements
have not generally been questioned. The latter
remain tied to a view of mental handicap as unable
and denoting a pathological condition which has an
objective existence of its own, rather than being
concerned with how we choose to respond to and

117

treat people who fail to reach criteria of normality.

Perceptions of mentally handicapped people still centre on differentness and inability where the concern is to treat, teach or care for them. We talk of mentally handicapped people, that is, their mental handicap comes first. Objectification becomes heightened as enthusiasm for the 'condition' increases and the notion of 'people' becomes left out altogether. Witness for example the frequency with which books and articles in the field refer to the 'mentally handicapped'. Mental handicap is turned from a description of a condition into a description of people who it is apparently assumed, represent an homogenous group because of their mental handicap. Certain characteristics, behaviours and needs are assumed simply because of membership of that group; otherwise there could never be a book entitled 'The Modern Management of Mental Handicap' (Simon 1980). Stereotyped ideas and responses do not reside merely in popular beliefs which professionals may criticise as based on ignorance; professionals themselves also engender stereotypes.

The public and media image of mental handicap is still dominated by fear of the unknown, pity for the deserving, or amazement that 'despite their handicaps' they can achieve some things for themselves. Society continues to insist that impairment is a mark of deviance, thus maintaining differences and handicapping conditions. Poignant indications of what the concept of mental handicap means in society at large are provided when people labelled as mentally handicapped are given the opportunity to say what it feels like. The following comments were recorded at a workshop organised by the Norfolk Campaign for People with Mental Handicaps (1983):

> They need to understand what it's like to be mentally handicapped.
> You've made us different.
> It's as if you don't belong.
> Scared we might attack them, though we never would.

However, as Bercovici (1983) noted, the stigma attached to mental handicap, and the perception as less than human, are not inevitable. Ideas, concepts and beliefs about mental handicap have been handed down to present generations, and they

are created and recreated in the material provisions surrounding people with mental handicaps,
those who care for them and provide services for
them. As teachers in special education for
children with severe learning difficulties, we and
the children we teach are not in any way immune to
such ideas, concepts and beliefs, however much we
would like to feel that we are. Present day situations and practices in special schools do not exist
in a vacuum. What goes on in school is connected
to attitudes, practices and provisions outside of
school; to social, economic and political factors
impinging on schools; to attitudes and provision
for people with mental handicaps; and to historical
events and circumstances in which other social,
economic and political forces played their part.

We said at the beginning of this book that we
were aiming to challenge taken for granted beliefs
and lay bare implicit assumptions and value
judgements, thereby provoking thought and
generating debate in an area of education which has
hitherto been characterised by a lack of critical
analysis. Our own analysis in the book so far has
concentrated upon the pupil-teacher relationship
and what is seen to constitute education and
teaching for children with severe learning
difficulties. Perceptions of children with severe
learning difficulties, of education and teaching,
are intricately linked to ideas and material
circumstances outside of the education system and
to issues of power and control. Critical analysis
of present educational practice for these children,
and arguing for alternative concepts of education
and teaching must therefore involve more than just
looking in depth at one's own ways of working and
what the direct consequences are for the children
concerned. It must involve a much deeper and more
acute grasp of the situations which teachers and
children with severe learning difficulties find
themselves in if they are together going to find
ways of substantially changing those situations.

In this sense critical analysis is something
which we are demanding must constantly take place.
It is not an exercise that one participates in a
few times a year after school, like curriculum
development meetings. Critical analysis involves
thinking discriminatively about what is actually
going on, why and how, and seeing and acting on the
implications which are revealed in all the spheres
of activity in which we as teachers participate.
Teachers, as individuals, can personally alter

their working relationships with pupils inside their classrooms, but this may represent merely a cosmetic change because of the circumstances and situations children are faced with outside of a One-to-One relationship with a particularly sensitive and empathetic teacher. On the teacher's side, she may find herself labelled by colleagues and others as a fanatical eccentric who is tolerated but whose ideas and views are not really taken seriously. Speaking from personal experience, the latter position is one in which it is extremely difficult to maintain a stance which is at odds with predominant views and ways of working.

We don't see this book as providing answers for teachers in dealing with the difficulties associated with working in schools for children with severe learning difficulties, the various pressures placed upon them which constrain their ways of working, or the contradictory demands being made of them in practice. We are not suggesting that there is either a solution to the dilemma of whether individual action, at the level of pupil-teacher interaction, will have any significant long term effect on the life chances of children with severe learning difficulties and future mentally handicapped people, or the demoralisation teachers feel when they see their work of many months being undone in situations outside of their control.

If anything the issues that have been raised, and the possibilities for change involved in viewing education from a different perspective, suggest more questions and elucidate further contradictions. For example, a process and rights oriented concept of education stands in contradiction to the compulsory nature of schooling and the social control function it serves. Furthermore, there are inherent inequalities between teachers and pupils because education is compulsory and because some are adults and some are children. Talking about teaching as facilitation does not get rid of such inequalities, it merely highlights them. Other difficulties raised by emphasising the rights of children with severe learning difficulties and mentally handicapped people are what happens when a child or young person does not want to participate, and refuses point blank to interact? What constitutes his rights in such a situation? For teachers who presently consider children as having significant rights in schools and in being educated, there are contradictions between children's rights and parents' rights, and being an employee responsible for implementing legislation and policy in classrooms, anyway.

There are two predominant sets of issues which teachers must confront. One set is to do with understanding and coming to terms with why things are as they are, and the other involves how, as teachers, we can act upon this knowledge to challenge and change the way things are. If teachers are concerned about what is happening, and why, they need to address themselves to the specific consequences of the nature of categorisation and labelling, the social interests involved in the field of special education, and the political nature of the education system.

BECOMING A MENTALLY HANDICAPPED PERSON

Within the caring professions it is generally held that identification and categorisation of people who have needs over and above or different from those currently provided for within the mainstream of society, is adminstratively and legally necessary for services to be demanded and then provided to meet those needs and to plan future services. In the case of mental handicap the individual has a particular set of difficulties resulting from his condition. Identifying him as a child with severe learning difficulties, or mentally handicapped, means that services can be provided as a direct response to the individual's characteristics and therefore the problems he has. It all seems a natural response to individual needs.

However, categorisation is itself a social activity in that any idea of disability and/or handicap is relative to ideas about what constitutes normality. In this sense the label 'mentally handicapped' is not an objective description of a person's needs, it is someone else's interpretation of their condition in the context of the societal structure of the time, and all the implications that structure has for defining what mental handicap is, and what normality is. Categorisation and labelling therefore involves professionals' value judgements about others, and are linked to perceptions and assumptions which have their basis in past attitudes and beliefs, historical events and material circumstances.

Furthermore it can be argued that differentiation and categorisation has far more to

do with meeting needs other than those of the
people so labelled. For example, in categorising
children as having special educational needs, the
needs of mainstream schooling are served by
removing difficult children, thus allowing special
education to act as a safety valve for mainstream
education (Tomlinson 1981, 1982). Professionals'
vested interests are served by differentiation and
categorisation of people with disabilities, and a
whole service industry has been developed around
disability and handicap serving important economic
and political interests (Farber 1968, Scull 1977,
Finkelstein 1980).

Seeing mentally handicapped people as having
special needs and requiring differential responses
from so-called normal people cannot therefore ever
be understood simply as a 'natural' result of
society acknowledging a pre-existing condition.
There are other issues involved besides the
individual's 'condition', and in any case mental
handicap is only a 'condition' because we choose to
identifying it as such.

Part of the difficulty in grasping that
labelling children as having severe learning
difficulties involves serious social issues and is
itself a social process, lies in the fact that
categories and labels attached to people become
interpreted as definitions of them, reified as
'truth', as 'reality'. As Bogdan and Kugelmass
point out:

> People come to believe that children actually
> ... have I.Q.s, and are mentally retarded or
> emotionally disturbed

instead of remembering that such categories:

> ... are ways of thinking about others,
> attitudes we take towards them, ways of
> structuring relationships and accepted
> processes and frames of mind. ...Disability
> counts and definitions are reifications of
> customs and practice (Bogdan and Kugelmass
> 1984, pp. 183 - 184).

The label mental handicap itself becomes
endowed with an objective existence. Its social
origins, in terms of being about people's
perceptions of each other, become hidden from view
and forgotten alongside other needs being served
through the categorisation process. This happens

both because of the reasons why categorisation is occurring, the way and form in which it is carried out, and the consequences which ensue. For people with mental handicaps in England at the moment, the reasons for categorisation made explicit and expressed in professional ideology, are to identify their needs. The way in which categorisation is carried out is predominantly by medical and psychological professionals on individuals. The form categorisation takes is that behavioural characteristics are characterised as relating to an underlying condition affecting people and having broadly homogenous results identifying them as a specific group. The consequences are provision of services in response to the identified need as it is manifested as a property of the condition, and hence the label under which the person is categorised.

Within this process there is little room for argument about who is being categorised by whom and for what purpose, and what the unintended consequences of that process might be. The individual himself certainly has no say in it, and professional expertise, authority and power induces parents and other professionals (especially those lower down the status ladder such as teachers and paramedics) to take for granted that those involved in the categorisation and labelling process are acting in the best interests of the child.

The severity of impairment and the difficulties families and individuals are faced with make it even harder not to see mental handicap as the individual's condition, and not to see labelling it as such and providing specialist services as a neutral process. Discoveries by the medical world of definite aetiological factors associated with severe mental handicap, such as various chromosonal abnormalities, metabolic disorders, pre- and peri-natal factors, and some childhood diseases, have directly helped to confirm the assertion that severe mental handicap is an objective category which has underlying physiological causes, whereas mild mental handicap may be acknowledged as more frequently being the result of 'environmental deprivation' or lack of stimulation. Similarly, the discoveries of direct cures for some metabolic disorders previously associated with severe mental handicap, such as phenylketonuria, have helped maintain the idea that mental handicap is ostensibly 'incurable' until more remarkable medical discoveries are made. This has further strengthened the idea of severe mental handicap as static, in a similar way to the IQ fatalism originally preached in the early 1900s but still influential in defining the degree of mental handicap. For example, although a severely mentally handicapped person may learn many self-help skills, and be able to read and write, he won't usually ever be re-categorised; he keeps his label for life. The medical model thus asserts that in the case of severe mental handicap, education and training may ameliorate certain symptoms, but it will not affect the cause, which is pathological.

If teachers are to take on board the idea of people with mental handicaps having the same rights and needs as the rest of us and understand fully the implications of this stance, they must develop their own critical awareness of the social nature of categorisation and labelling. They must be able to question seriously and counteract the dominance of the medical model of mental handicap in their own attitudes and approaches to children with severe learning difficulties and in the definition of education, what constitutes teaching and how children with severe learning difficulties should be taught.

Categorisation and labelling not only serve the purpose of providing a useful description but also imply an understanding of cause, course of action to be taken, prognosis and a conceptual framework for interpreting and making sense of behaviour. In this way, the label 'severe mental handicap' has gained credibility as both a description of a person, and an explanation of them. Cause and effect become the same thing - behaviour is put down as a result of mental handicap, and the mental handicap is identified by the behaviour. Within the framework of such ideas the word

> ... mental retardation ... makes us selectively sensitive to certain behaviours and actions. Things that might not have been noticed before, jump out and take on meaning ... Behaviour and physical characteristics that were noted and interpreted in one way, get interpreted in another way ... (Bogdan and Kugelmass 1984 p. 186).

Teachers must be aware of this happening in their own practice and be able to combat it.

Maureen Oswin tells the story of Shirley sitting on the long stay ward playing with her tears: "One of the visitors said, 'These children are cabbages', and the others agreed with him, but perhaps it hadn't occurred to them to look at Shirley and consider that cabbages don't cry" (Oswin in Shearer 1981 p. 83). At present too often we are not sensitive or perceptive. Our ability to listen, to observe, to make sense of, to understand and act on that understanding are not usually seen as at issue. Think for example how common it still is for headteachers to show visitors around classrooms pointing to so and so who has such and such problems, and how often teachers themselves will discuss children's difficulties and inabilities in front of them as if they aren't there or assuming that they are impervious to such comments because they are 'too thick' to understand them. Perhaps they might not understand everything but it is still an insult to their humanity and denies them the respect due to all people.

Knowledge is a significant factor involved in teachers being in a position to think critically and reflect on their practice. Being able to develop an acute sense of the current meaning of mental handicap, the values and assumptions it is tied in with, is helped by viewing it as intricately linked to why and how present services are organised and provided. This becomes clearer when viewed in the context of how the present service system developed.

Things are changing. The social climate of the 1970s brought forth both the Warnock (1978) and Jay (1979) reports, with their high sounding rhetoric as the way forward. Service provision of certain types and in certain geographical areas is ostensibly radically different to that offered by the colonies to the mental defectives of previous years, and there are some schemes which offer real integration within the community. However, the perceptions of pity on the one hand, and fear on the other, remain alongside massive segregation and deprivation at all levels. Mentally handicapped people are a minority group who occupy marginal status. They are the subject of stereotyped images and responses, both at the level of institutions and from other individuals. At the moment a mentally handicapped person does not have the same rights as other members of the community. As Wertheimer (1981) points out, this group is one of the most severely disadvantaged, stigmatised and

125

segregated amongst people with disabilities. The most common expression of the denial of the mentally handicapped person's rights, apart from the still gross levels of institutionalisation, must be in the lack of respect afforded, for example by denying privacy, or by continual treatment as for ever childlike.

Even when faced with the activities of people with mental handicaps in the self-advocacy movement, the retort of many, public and professionals alike, is that it is only the most able that are involved, implying that many mentally handicapped people are not and will not be capable of self advocacy in the same way. Another excuse for not taking self-advocacy seriously is the idea that particular professionals are behind groups and have and are using them as mouthpieces, probably for political ends, implying that in fact mentally handicapped people are not speaking for themselves, are not expressing their own ideas and interests. A further excuse is that they may have their own views, and should be encouraged to express them, but what they say must be taken with a pinch of salt, because they are 'mentally handicapped', and professionals know best what their needs are, and how those needs should be met in the long term.

During the last two centuries, movements and ideas within the social, economic and political climates of the time, bore directly upon provision for mentally handicapped children and adults, and played their part in an emerging concept of mental handicap which was and still is epitomised by the conflict between protecting society and protecting mentally handicapped people, and giving a humane face to segregation and institutionalisation.

In trying to understand the development of service provision, Wolfensberger (1969) draws attention to the conflicting roles which have been (and continue to be) assigned to mentally handicapped people by society generally, and by those persons who are in positions of responsibility for mentally handicapped people. These roles reflect the contradictory ideas that make up a concept of mental handicap, since so far none has dominated over and above the others:
(1) the intended benign role which seeks compassion and tolerance for the individual's disability, but ascribes to the idea of the 'poor innocent' and maintains the individual in a permanent state of dependence;
(2) the malign role where hostile and devaluing

attitudes are expressed towards the individual's disability and his inhuman-ness is stressed along with its harmful consequences for others;
(3) the actual benign role where the existence of disability is neither denied or over-emphasised and opportunities are arranged for the individual to develop his abilities.

The notions expressed in these three typified sets of attitudes and ascriptions penetrate the ideas and movements present during the establishment of specific and segregated provision for mentally handicapped people during the nineteenth century. What must be stressed, is firstly the conflicts involved between different roles, and therefore the diverse interests and purposes to be served by material practices and provisions; and secondly the importance of social forces in the shape of political and economic circumstances of the time, and the ideas of individuals and groups of people who were able to establish the development of certain courses of action, rather than others. Direct consequences for mentally handicapped people did, and still do, result in terms of both social policy on a national scale, and ways of interacting with mentally handicapped people on a personal scale, because of the delineation of mental handicap as a 'problem' in the public's eyes, and as a case for 'treatment' in professional circles.

Both compounding segregation, and resulting from it, has been the continual emphasis during the twentieth century on the differences between 'them and us'. The optimism and apparent humanism of the early nineteenth century pioneers was overshadowed by the fashionable movements of social Darwinism and Eugenics, the medical and psychological professions' claim of 'scientific objectivity' and the economic efficiency debates about the feasibility of providing education and training for those who would not be able to pay back society. From then on there were no more public references to the humanity of mental defectives in their sharing of potentially the same human qualities as others more fortunate. Rather their inhumanity was stressed and used to legitimate inhumane treatment.

The kind of arguments which suggest 'they don't know any better', 'they're happier with their own kind', 'they live in their own worlds, they don't understand feelings the way we do, they don't have feelings like us', came into their own in justifying 'specialist' provision which was

127

characterised by segregation and deprivation of
basic facilities and rights which most of us take
for granted. Furthermore, differentness has been
continually associated, during this century, with
negative connotations, both because of the very
ideas which led to mental handicap being recognised
initially and because of the actual provisions
which were then set up to deal with the
acknowledged problem. A consideration of some of
the words used to refer to mentally handicapped
people, spanning both official terminology and
colloquialisms, is revealing in that the emphasis
is on 'what is missing' and on using descriptive
terms which conjure up set images including notions
of ugliness, danger, perversion and stupidity. For
example - moron, imbecile, mentally subnormal,
witless, simple, half-baked, not all there, brain-
less, cracked, cretin, cuckoo, barmy, clodhopper,
loon. These words are expressive of the then
emerging concept of mental handicap as referring to
people who aren't 'people' in the ordinary sense.
This same line of thinking is evident today in
professional terminology. Although they may sound
nicer, words and phrases like severe learning
difficulties, mental age, low grade, behaviourally
disturbed, attention seeking, behaviour management
and so on, are still fundamentally 'them and us'
words and detract from the humanity of the people
they are aimed at. Thomas notes that:

> ... among the problems confronting disabled
> people is the perception of both lay and
> professional people. Such perceptions may be
> ....re-coded and re-emerge as new labels or
> slogans which give rise to the illusion of
> progress while leaving the basic structure of
> perception and behaviour unchanged, so that
> the rhetoric of acceptance and normalisation
> may not be translated into a social reality
> (Thomas 1982, p. 173).

In thinking critically about education and
teaching, teachers must take into account that
becoming one of the 'mentally handicapped' is an
intricate social process which goes far beyond the
differentiation of a person from others on the
grounds of his intellectual disability. One of the
most significant characteristics of the labelling
process in the construction of the identity of a
mentally handicapped person is the way the label is
over-generalised. Mental handicap has become a

holistic term referring to the whole person. Phrases such as 'the mentally handicapped' are depersonalising and objectifying because of this association with the whole person and because they, being symptomatic of the negativity and rigidity with which the present concept of mental handicap is endowed, place the emphasis on the handicap, the non-person, rather than the human being involved. As Shearer suggests:

> ... people who have cerebral palsy become the 'spastics'; people who are mentally retarded, 'the subnormal'; people who have arthritis, 'the arthritics'. By turning a description of a condition into a description of people, we are saying that this is all we really need to know about them. We confirm their abnormality (Shearer 1981, p. 3).

The medical model and the view of mentally handicapped people as deficit systems and therefore the assumption that 'they can't' and 'won't ever' are intricately tied into current service provision, and predominate almost to the point of precluding the presentation of alternative ideas and strategies for practice.

In special education for children with severe learning difficulties Bart points out that:

> Seldom does one hear about special children's aspirations, contributions or potential, or how these qualities are developed or stymied by current educational practice. This is because the terms of the field are the language of management, not education, and they suggest that there is something awry, something to manage (Bart 1984, p. 93).

The excuse is always that the line has been trodden between denying and not denying 'handicap', between protecting the individual, and protecting others; but the result is that mental handicap is used to justify the limitation of rights.

EDUCATION AND CHILDREN WITH SEVERE LEARNING DIFFICULTIES - POLITICS AND SOCIAL INTERESTS

In order to understand why things are as they are, we further need to come to terms with the fact that the education system, and the practice of education for children with severe learning difficulties, is full of conflicting ideas and demands, and competing ideologies. The rhetoric preached in government papers, Acts of Parliament, and policy documents of authorities does not provide an accurate description of what actually happens when making available specialist educational provision. Rather the reality is altogether more messy and complex.

Special education is itself a social process, set within a political and economic context. The special needs of children with severe learning difficulties are related to ' ... the public issues as to why a society decides to separate, however minimally, and in whatever way, children who are special from children who are normal' (Tomlinson 1982, p. 182). Severe learning difficulty and mental handicap must be understood in terms of common sense assumptions and value judgements, about what people are supposed to be able to do, and about what is valued in society - success, prosperity, competitive effort, intelligence, physique, beauty and so on. As Bogdan and Kugelmass say:

> Some problems are technical - providing physical access to wheelchairs, building communication systems for non-verbal people - other problems are moral and social. They are located much deeper in the seams of our society, than professionals in the field of special education touch (Bogdan and Kugelmass 1984, p. 189).

All children's entitlement to an appropriate education which is geared to their needs, appears to be given priority in recent Education Acts and government documents about the curriculum. It is acknowledged that all children have abilities and disabilities, and most from time to time experience difficulties, but some children are still singled out and provided with a different legal framework for education because their problems are 'greater or more persistent' (DES 1980, p. 10). Attention continues to be focused on certain children's difficulties and disabilities, not upon the failure of the ordinary system to cope, and the reasons why it rejects children who do not fit into ordinary facilities. The assumption remains that the difficulty lies within the child. The continued provision of special education in special schools for children with severe learning difficulties is a response to the severity of what is seen as their

handicap. It confirms the perception of them as
fundamentally different from other people, still
objects of pity and fear, and still pawns, at the
level of legal definitions, organisation and
provision of services, because of the powerful
conflicts of interests and contradictory purposes
involved.

The non-position of children with severe
learning difficulties in the debate about integration in education is a case in point. In fact the
government are quite blunt about their reasons:
'... in the present economic circumstances, there
is no possibility of finding the massive additional
resources ... which would be required to enable
every ordinary school to provide an adequate education for children with serious educational difficulties' (DES, 1980 p. 13). But of course there
are other reasons too. Uppermost among them are
professionals' vested interests both in special
education and mainstream schools. The interests
and needs of children themselves do not necessarily
play a primary role.

Dominant at present in the rhetoric of the
establishment is the ideology that 'Education ...
is a good, and a specifically human good to which
all human beings are entitled' (Warnock 1978 1:7).
However the professed universality of the major
aims of education, as well as reinforcing the
ideology of education as a good in itself, show at
once that the 'good' is not simply for the
individual, but also for the 'whole'. This
includes interests outside of the individual, which
affect him, and which he in turn may affect as a
member of the community. Schooling is at one and
the same time, therefore, about education in terms
of the development of individual capabilities,
knowledge and understanding, and about training
children in terms of socialisation. The dominant
conception of education as a means to an end -
employment and the ratification of individual differences and levels of achievement, providing a
meritocratic means to 'occupational success, social
mobility, privilege and advancement' (Tomlinson
1982, p. 6) - confirms the major function of the
education system as social control. In the first
instance then, the purpose of compulsory education
embodies, at least potentially, although many argue
in reality, conflicts of interest between individuals and other interests in society such as the
requirements of industry and the need for social
stability.

Special education defined in terms of needs rather than categories of handicap, has enabled the benevolent rhetoric of education as a personal good to be further entrenched in educational policy, directing attention away from the possibility that needs other than those of the children may be being met. It has further enabled special education for children with severe learning difficulties to continue to be embedded in the definitional system of the medical model, and saturated by the ideology of management in the guise of education. The rhetoric of official policy assumes that special education is a neutral process. Bart (1984) uses the phrase ' naturalising' to describe this process as it refers to what happens in categorising children for special education and the predominant processes of practice which then occur. These involve the same line of thinking about diagnosis and categorisation of the difficulty or 'need' of the child, the way that process occurs with reference to the child's lack, deficiency, problem, and the consequent utilisation of methods and resources to remedy the fault, or compensate for it.

The ideas that categorisation and labelling are essentially social activities, that social forces are deeply involved in identity construction, that services occur within a social milieu and are therefore influenced by social, economic and political factors, are not new. Yet there has been very little consideration of the economic, political and social factors involved in the construction of mental handicap in the field in general (examples are Booth 1978; Goode 1984); little consideration of the social nature of special education (examples are Barton and Tomlinson 1981, 1984; Tomlinson 1982); and even less consideration of the social nature of the special education system as it applies to children with severe learning difficulties.

At the level of discussing the maintenance of handicapping conditions for people with disabilities, it is nearly always people with physical disabilities that are the concern, for example in discussing access. When special education is discussed in relation to the problematic nature of assessment and the referral system, and the possiblity that special education may actually compound children's difficulties, children with emotional or behavioural difficulties and children with moderate (not severe) learning difficulties are singled out as the groups where social forces rather than an objective special educational need, may be at work in the labelling and categorisation process.

Only when the rhetoric has begun to be untangled is it clear that other considerations come to the fore in the provision of schooling for children with severe learning difficulties today, just as they did at its inception in removing difficult children from mainstream classes, and just as they are concerned in the provision of schooling for any pupil. One of the primary motivations is still that children with severe learning difficulties, despite being very slow learners, can, with '... appropriate techniques and skilled teachers, be taught basic social and personal skills which would equip them to live at home, rather than be cared for permanently and more expensively in an institution' (Topliss 1982, pp. 117-118).

We would contend that the 1981 Education Act has not provided a framework which alters the dominant balance of interests in favour of individual needs, despite the emphasis on special educational needs rather than on categories of handicap as the baseline for provision. The Act typifies how special education legislation is both enabling and controlling. As with all legislation, the concern is with accountability, and the 1981 Act ensures that '... special educational needs are met, and met in a way that safeguards the child, the parents and the community - the taxpayer...' (Welton et al. 1982, p. 15).

Legislation concerned with education has not generally been revolutionary in advocating change. It has merely legitimated and justified the ideas and educational thinking which are already beginning to be put into practice, and has provided the legal framework necessary to enforce certain priorities. As Welton et al. say, the 1981 Education Act is a good example of '... amending legislation made necessary by changes in opinion and practice about the ... way of providing for special educational needs' (Welton et al. 1982, p. 14). It doesn't challenge the basic assumptions embodied in the system, and the conflicting ideologies and interests involved which ensure the priority of more powerful interests - such as economic efficiency, productive use of resources and maintenance of the status quo - over and above the needs of individuals. Instead, the needs of

individuals are entangled with other interests in
benevolent rhetoric which presents a picture of
them being the same thing.

Special education as it developed alongside
the general education system, has been providing a
sorting and containing function for it and for
society at large; '... professionals have been
mandating the special child's fate in an arena
where "scientific expertise" has often functioned
to legitimise essentially moral decisions of social
and economic import' (Bart 1984 p. 9).

These are arguments which teachers of children
with severe learning difficulties need at least to
be aware of. Perhaps such arguments do not tell
the whole story, and oversimplify a complexity of
factors. As teachers we have to make our own minds
up as to which side of the fence we are on. The
point is that such arguments have very serious
implications for what we are doing both to and for
children. To be unaware of their significance is
dangerously naive and professionally irresponsible.
If teachers want to be involved in substantially
changing the opportunities and life circumstances
available to children with severe learning difficulties and to mentally handicapped people, they
need not only to know what they might be taking on,
but to understand fully why they want to challenge
and change present circumstances.

In highlighting some of the major issues which
must be considered in understanding why things are
as they are, we hope to have ensured that teachers
are alert to some of the questions they must face
if they are to participate in a re-evaluation of
education and teaching which is realistic instead
of naively looking at teaching methods and
curriculum content in a vacuum. What maintains
handicapping conditions and negative perceptions of
people with mental handicaps? How is education
both implicated and creative in this process? How
is it that we exchange one set of labels for
another which convince us that we have
fundamentally changed our underlying assumptions
and values, yet the consequences remain
substantially unaltered? Why does the medical
model of mental handicap still have such a
stranglehold on educational practice? And not
least, what does the current conception of
education for children with severe learning
difficulties do to teachers? Are they being
deskilled? Are they really also dehumanised

alongside their pupils by the mechanical and rigid approach to teaching?

TOWARDS CHANGE

Present practice and current trends in the education of children with severe learning difficulties have been criticised by a few people who have put forward very positive conceptions of learning difficulty and mental handicap, and different ideas about teaching, methodology, and content (for example Stevens 1976; Sherbourne 1979; Goddard 1983; Heathcote 1981; Serpell-Morris 1982). However, as yet any explicit theoretical framework within which alternative concepts and practice are derived, is lacking. Even though people like Stevens and Sherbourne have emphasised working upon a sound theoretical base, this has tended to be simply generalised theory of child development. As Stevens says herself '... I have adopted in the main what I feel is sound from current thought about child development, and progressive education generally' (Stevens 1976, p. 12). Stevens, along with others, falls into the same trap as the supporters of the skills analysis paradigm, in that the components of 'normal' child development become the objectives of teaching, so that they are in effect trying to teach development. The children's position as 'mentally handicapped' is still confirmed by the comparison to 'normal' child development and the use of it as a yardstick for education.

The only forum in which the rights of people with mental handicaps are really being seen as at issue is in the self-advocacy movement, and where normalisation has been developed as a coherent framework for practice incorporating rights to participation in planning and implementing services. However, it should be noted that the self-advocacy movement can itself be seen as contradictory in some respects because of the process of identification it involves of mentally handicapped people as a minority group, while at the same time proclaiming that needs and rights are the same as other people's.

Normalisation, according to Wolfensberger, is about creating and supporting socially valued roles within society for people who are at present in devalued positions. As a principle of action normalisation covers areas such as role expectancies, social imagery, participation and use of culturally valued means in order to enable

135

people to be valued as community members (Wolfensberger and Thomas 1981). This involves a great deal more than increasing devalued persons' competencies and their ability to cope with more normal surroundings, or placing them in environments which look more normal to the outsider. But creating more normal appearances and improving functional skills are what has been called normalisation in England (Tyne 1981).

In the education of children with severe learning difficulties, normalisation is not usually referred to as a guiding principle. However, in the movement towards the objective and skills analysis approach, the idea that the resultant educational programme is in line with normalisation as a policy for provision for mentally handicapped people, is implicit because of the emphasis placed on independence as an aim. But as we have argued, the objectives/skills analysis paradigm embodies a very narrow concept of skills and competence and is representative of precisely the misunderstanding of normalisation Wolfensberger criticises, i.e. normalising children, not environments and attitudes. As we have pointed out, 'making children more normal' is often explicitly stated as an aim in curriculum policy and educational programme planning. It is not simply that this is a fundamental misconception of the normalisation principle, it is also that the skills of independence emphasised are those of normal appearances, rather than those of participation in the processes of living most of us take for granted.

The fact that social issues and social construction are significant aspects in concepts of severe learning difficulty and mental handicap, and provision of services and practices involved, shows that concepts and practices are not in any way simply products of the evolution of knowledge. The assumptions and values embedded in dominant concepts and present practice can be challenged, provision can be changed and discrimination guarded against. This is not to say that in this case there aren't difficulties and problems involved in teachers trying to take on different ways of working based on different values and assumptions, or that their changed practice in interaction with children with severe learning difficulties will automatically lead to changes at the level of educational policy and in the social world outside of school. However, it is to say that the tenets of a framework for change must incorporate a broader view than what is or isn't seen as good teaching practice inside the classroom. Different levels and spheres of action are involved from the relationship between pupil and teacher, between teachers and children, and between teachers, parents and children; the inter-relations between staff and headteacher and with the LEA; through to spheres of activity outside of school boundaries, in government circles, in the public mind and in the community in which children live.

Possibilities for change may arise from the process of critical reflection and the instigation of debate. We can only make suggestions here as to what these possibilities might entail when different levels of action and practice are incorporated because of the links and contradictions between action at an individual level and the structure of society. The latter can negate the former in a very real way outside of any momentary interaction between people (e.g. Goode 1984; Bart 1984). This isn't because of any overt conspiracy by policy makers and planners, or the powers that be. Rather it is an expression of the complexity of human action and societal response and the role of unintended consequences.

Wolfensberger and Thomas' (1981) explanation of normalisation theory, in the terms of seven core themes, provides us with a more concise idea of the extent of the issues to be confronted in striving to understand the position of devalued people and develop alternative ways of thinking, different ways of acting and practising in providing services which will begin to give children with severe learning difficulties and mentally handicapped people socially valued roles.

In relation to the education system, these seven core themes entail firstly considering the role of (un)consciousness in educational organisation and practice. We have continually referred to the underlying dynamics of educational policy and practice in terms of implicit assumptions, taken for granted values and beliefs, and their role in framing provision for and actions towards children with severe learning difficulties. In order for the negative and destructive impact of these to be lessened, in the experiences of children with severe learning difficulties, they must be made explicit. Professionals and those planning and administering education must work within a conscious appraisal of the values underlying interaction with children with severe underlying interaction with children with severe learning difficulties, and provision of services for them. There are techniques which can help people become more consciously aware of their own attitudes and beliefs which are being employed in training workshops on normalisation in England by organisations such as CMHERA (The Community and Mental Handicap Educational and Research Association) and MIND. The service evaluation instruments 'PASS' and 'PASSING', developed to examine provision and practices with regard to the implementation of normalisation and the acknowledgement of people's rights, are specifically structured to rate highly consciousness on the part of service personnel (Wolfensberger and Thomas 1981; Dickens 1984). Tyne notes that CMHERA's experience in systematically teaching people about some of the 'more commonly destructive dynamics, e.g. treating mentally handicapped adults as non-humans, or as children or as sick, or as a threat, or as trivia' (Tyne 1981, p. 25) helped people recognise these dynamics in their own work so that they could' ... plan and implement rational strategies for avoiding them' (Tyne 1981, pp. 25-26). Obviously it is not just face to face workers who need to examine their values and beliefs. DES and local authority personnel, elected members of Educational Committees, governors and those involved in policy making and planning the development of services, need to examine the assumptions upon which those services are and will be based. Teachers can and should play an active role in ensuring that this happens.

A second major theme of normalisation is concerned with role expectancy and role circularity. Wolfensberger and Thomas point out that:

> There are at least five major kinds of circumstances which can convey role expectancies to a person. These include the way the physical environment is structured, the activities that are offered to, provided for, or demanded of a person, the language that is used to and about the person, the people who are placed with the person, and miscellaneous other imagery and symbolism that may convey any number of messages (Wolfensberger and Thomas 1981, p. 14).

In the case of children with severe learning difficulties, their place in the special education system and the kind of experience they are offered in school, from the locks on the doors to curriculum content, suggests negative expectancies and confirms devalued roles.

The identification of positive roles and expectancies for children with severe learning difficulties is involved in reversing this position. In school and in interaction in the classroom positive roles such as student, friend, chairperson, participant, helper can be identified. Other implications with regard to the organisation of the special education system, the institutional structures of schools, the use of language, involve questioning the purpose and form of assessing special educational needs, the participation of those involved - children, parents and teachers - in the decision making process and in the control of the education offered.

The multiplying effect of the disabilities of both individuals and groups, and the power of imitation are further significant tenets of normalisation theory which have implications for practice within schools and within the special education system. The more skills and competencies a person has, the more likely it is that differences and/or deviance will be tolerated. Conversely, seeing an individual's disabilities in the context of a group of similarly disabled people can increase the appearance of difference and the impact of deviance so that it is less likely to be tolerated and more likely to lead to negative re- actions. The grouping together of children with severe learning difficulties in separate schools multiplies the handicapping effect of special edu- cation. Taking large groups of children out in minibuses, which proclaim their differences by the writing on the sides, similarly portrays the image of them as not like others, thus creating handicap out of disability. The segregation of children with severe learning difficulties in special schools further means that they have little access to positive role models provided by peers who occupy socially valued roles. The separateness and isolation of special schooling and the stigma attached to it is therefore implicated as well as the negative influence on the children of being surrounded by others who display equally negatively valued attributes of behaviour and incompetence, and by teachers too if they adhere to the role of expert and imposer in interaction with them and their families.

Personal competency enhancement is the theme

of normalisation which the skills analysis paradigm mistakenly latches on to as meaning that if children with severe learning difficulties acquire sufficient skills and a high enough level of competence they will become independent and accepted in the community. We have already noted that this is unrealistic and ignores the adaptations and supports needed to circumvent disabilities in providing services, and the changes necessary in societal structures and values underpinning them to allow for disability instead of discriminating against and devaluing the people concerned. Personal competency enhancement must therefore be viewed in the context of providing socially valued roles, rather than simplistically as the means to achieve those roles.

A negative social image of children with severe learning difficulties is also frequently portrayed in the special education system. The importance of social imagery in adding to de-valuation and discrimination means that in providing for valuation and non-discriminatory practice, things like the location of schools, the ages of the children catered for, the activities and methods used, the name of the school and the way pupils attending it are labelled, as well as how they are referred to in groupings within the school, and the way the school projects its public image (for example in avoiding pity imagery) must all be taken into consideration, especially in terms of the differences imposed on the experiences of children with severe learning difficulties in comparison to their peers. Tyne notes that:

> Awareness of issues to do with ... imagery is typically minimal among service providers. For example, the administrators of a large northern hospital who recently selected a badger as a logo for the hospital, and the service it provides, may be unaware that in rural areas badgers are classified as vermin which should be exterminated, or at best as a rare species which should be preserved, but in zoos or similar custodial settings (Tyne 1981, p. 29).

The final theme of normalisation involves the argument that 'Integration into the life of normal society should be social and not just physical, i.e. involve socially valued participation' (Lishman 1981, p. 7). This argument doesn't simply refer to the physical segregation of children with severe learning difficulties in special schools and the activities offered by the school, for example in using predominantly separate rather than integrated facilities such as swimming pools, playgrounds, sports halls. It also refers to the participation of children and young people in their education in terms of developing their own knowledge and understanding, making their own decisions so that they are respected as self determining people with the same rights as others.

The themes of normalisation make it clear that an approach to education which upholds the rights and entitlements of individuals as paramount goes beyond the four walls of the classroom and involves action at levels other than that of the teacher-pupil relationship. We would add that this involves treating yourself as a person with rights and entitlements, believing that you have a positive contribution to make,that teachers just like pupils, have a right to a level of self determination in their work, and therefore that others - children and colleagues - should treat you accordingly.

It is not simply the children whose opportunities are limited and who are subject to depersonalising and objectifying practices. Teachers are as much recipients of the system in which they work as children. Just as children with severe learning difficulties are dehumanised by present concepts of mental handicap and practices directly related to it, so too are teachers dehumanised by the instrumental view of education, of their job as teachers and in the demands made upon them to conform to particular ways of working and achieve specific end results. Teachers are continuously being told what they should be teaching, how and in what form. The educational psychologist tells them how to deal with behavioural management and classroom organisation, the government tells them what constitutes good practice, and curriculum packages even tell them what to say to children in particular lessons. It seems that teachers, like children with severe learning difficulties, are not treated as thinking human beings, respected as skilled people in their own right, with important ideas and valuable contributions to make. Instead they seem to be more and more constrained in their work, with increasingly diverse and contradictory demands being made of them (efficiency, quality, pupil achievements, order and control to name but a few), stemming from similarly diverse sources. If there ever was a time when education was the teacher's prerogative, that time is long since gone.

How do teachers get from ideas to actions?

As well as knowledge of why things are as they are and the changes that need to occur to alter substantially the consequences for children with severe learning difficulties, time, energy and commitment are involved in being able to think critically, reflect and then follow through the implications. Many teachers may understandably feel that they haven't got the time and energy to spend on critical analysis and reflection with regard to fundamental values, beliefs and ideas about what education is, apart from the practical day to day tasks they are faced with. This in itself creates a difficulty in calling for a re-evaluation of teaching and education which goes beyond teaching methods and curriculum content. We, as teachers, have to find ways of creating the space in which critical analysis can occur, and of reserving the energy to be able to do it.

Teachers may further see themselves as having little if any control or influence over some of the issues we have highlighted, or feel that they are constrained in what they can challenge and attempt to change because they have to maintain working relationships with their colleagues and superiors. On the other hand a great deal of time and energy is frequently expended in complaining and moaning about situations within our role as teachers which we may not be happy with, such as gripes at colleagues for their negative attitudes, or frustration at the latest edicts of the headteacher or the Local Education Authority to complete reports, schedules or schemes of work with which we disagree. Instead of moaning, it is up to teachers to develop strategies which will allow them more say in their working situations and from which a basis for change can be established.

Changing attitudes and the structure of ways of working is something that teachers can and do have influence over. However, as we have already indicated, as an individual on your own it is extremely difficult to maintain a stance which is at odds with dominant ideas. It can also be very demoralising. The effectiveness of an individual stance is questionable too, although in terms of the teacher's relationship with children and young people within her own sphere of teaching, it should not be underestimated; not least because of the possibilities of creating circumstances in which the children, both now and as future adults, can challenge situations they are faced with, for themselves. If teachers really want to start to get to grips with issues we have raised, the most basic strategic move to make is to identify allies and find ways of working together with others collectively to solve problems and create the circumstances in which change can occur. This is essential at all levels of action from within school and without because of the individual's need for support and encouragement in what she is doing. Simply by raising questions to do with rights and participation (let alone suggesting alternatives), issues of power, authority and control are implicated both in terms of the teachers' autonomy or lack of it within their working situations, and in terms of the position of pupils as recipients of special education. Furthermore, the current trends towards teacher evaluation and accountability may mean that teachers find their practice more constrained by outside pressures, definitions and limitations in the future. Teachers therefore need to find ways of working collectively to counteract the constraints placed upon them and the reactions that may be provoked by questioning dominant values and established ways of working. They must provide back-up support and supervision services for themselves which allow their talents and skills to be shared, to be used appropriately, and to be developed and extended.

What we are really saying boils down to a basic teaching strategy, i.e. initially ensuring a high possibility of success and establishing confidence and positive self-image rather than demanding too much, risking failure and reinforcing a negative self-image. Find out what there is to be worked with, developed and extended. Don't start by trying to remedy the deficits. Within school it may be that a teacher, as an individual, has to demonstrate the success of her approach for some time before she is taken seriously. This is the kind of situation that we have both had to contend with. In such a situation, the teacher needs to identify the children as her allies. However, there may be at least one other member of staff who will be sympathetic, if not in total agreement, and this can provide a teacher with much needed support and the basis of a more co-operative and therefore more powerful method of challenging those tenets of attitude, technique, organisation and approach which are handicapping the children for whom she is responsible.

This takes us on to developing ways of organising schools and ways of working within them which may be significantly different to dominant practices at present. For example, teachers may as a collective, identify their different skills and preferences and work out class groupings accordingly. Decision making within the school itself can be democratised by extending ideas about 'school councils' not just to the role of pupils in making their views known, but also to the role of teachers in speaking for themselves within their own workplace. Williams and Shoultz (1982) point out that the impact of self-advocacy is not so dependent on the abilities of people with mental handicaps to speak for themselves as upon others ability and willingness to listen. This isn't something that just applies to people with mental handicaps.

The way is also open for teachers to step outside of their immediate school situation and develop collaboration and support amongst colleagues in other schools and amongst other professions involved with children with severe learning difficulties, e.g. paramedical staff, educational psychologists, staff in ATCs. We have personally been involved in setting up and participating in local and Authority-wide support groups for professionals. Interested parties meet regularly to discuss difficulties and exchange information and views about how problems may be solved. Such support groups can be usefully formed, for example amongst those concerned with particular groups of children such as those with profound disabilities, or with particular age groups like the post-16's. Initially such groups may be wholly concerned with practical difficulties and solving the day to day problems in a 'tips for teachers' fashion. However, such an arena also provides a forum in which critical analysis and reflection on underlying values and assumptions can develop, if only through teachers and other pro-fessionals sharing their ideas about the actual task of educating children with severe learning difficulties, and being faced with choices in terms of how they may carry out their work. Once it is realised that there is a choice and therefore a decision to be taken, the way is open to challenge the basis upon which decisions are made.

Beyond their own colleagues, teachers do have access to people in positions of power in the education authority such as advisers and inspectors. The inclusion of such a person in a support group can add much credibility as well as a direct entrance to the power structure of the authority and a method of developing strong coalitions.

Within their sphere of work teachers can also be legitimately active' in terms of alerting parents to educational issues which have serious consequences for their sons and daughters, thereby helping parents to mobilise their own resources.

However, acting at levels over and above that of personal relationships with pupils not only entails teachers being able to put forward clear arguments and alert others to the alternatives that are available. It is crucial that they realise the implications of their own actions, for themselves and for the children they teach. Collective action within schools and support groups across schools and professionals will almost inevitably lead to teachers being viewed as participating in pressure groups. Accusations and threats may well follow because teachers will be seen as acting in a political fashion. They may be told it is not their place to enter into debate and discussion of issues which incorporate policy and organisation both within their own schools and at the level of Local Education Authority structure. They may be used as scapegoats and pressured to conform, perhaps to the point of decisions being taken to remove them from one area of responsibility to another. Even at the level of individual teaching relationships with children, emphasising children's rights and participation in making decisions may well lead to teachers being told they are irresponsible. Critics will fall back on what they see as the children's limited understanding and capabilities to cope, in suggesting that to raise children's expectations is dangerous, because it creates the very real possibility of disruption and negative consequences for them when in other spheres of life. Outside of school they may be expected to conform and not to participate in decisions about what goes on in their lives. In this context it is important to remember how much rights and participation are about power and teachers allowing children legitimately to have the power to affect their education. Teachers have to do this if they are going to allow children to act

independently and actively teach what independence
is really about. Given present societal
circumstances, children with severe learning
difficulties may have very few other opportunities
to act as self-determining people, and to develop
skills of decision making and self control.

Changing ways of working, relations of teaching and attitudes towards children with severe
learning difficulties is not something that can
happen overnight. It involves a long and weary
struggle, together with much frustration. Often,
in our own situations, we have felt there to be
insurmountable obstacles and pressures and have
been prepared to move out of the fields of education and mental handicap altogether. We still get
very low and depressed and extremely frustrated.
The one thing that has ensured we continue, is our
belief in children as people and our commitment to
offer them, regardless of the opposition we may
face, the opportunities which respect their rights
as human beings and enable them to develop as self-
determining individuals.

It is easy to fall back on the idea that in
order to achieve a substantial change in attitudes
towards people and how they value themselves and
others, a restructuring of society is necessary
first. As the education system appears to be predominantly determined by social, political and
economic considerations impinging on it, change at
the level of societal structure can be viewed as
necessary before reform in education becomes meaningful, rather than simply a reworking of present
discriminatory practice. Indeed, we do run the
risk of change in the education system being reac-
tionary and providing just a nicer, and more
acceptable way of maintaining the status quo and
reproducing a hierarchical structure, where mentally handicapped people become the 'also rans',
positioned on the periphery of society as a marginal group with marginal status. As well as identifying spheres where action must occur, for example
at the level of the individual teacher, her primary
and intermediate social systems (family and local
community, school), and at the level of societal
systems (law, public awareness, attitudes,
imagery), teachers must also take into account and
be consciously aware that:

> ... Potentially radical educational demands,
> arising from liberal-democratic ideology, are
> accommodated to an educational system that

remains functional to the needs of a corporate economy ... Special Education reform ... may proceed only to the extent that it is congruent with the needs or goals of that structure (Shapiro 1980, p. 212).

Our own stance clearly shows that we do not believe that education is a totally determined system and that people within it are compelled to treat each other in prescribed ways. If teachers want to recognise the rights and place of children with severe learning difficulties as people like other individuals, then they have to confront their responsibility for their own perceptions and practices. We have to implement change ourselves. We can't wait for public attitudes and societal values to change to accommodate children with severe learning difficulties without discriminating against them. But at the same time we need to grasp the social, political and economic implications of different values and changed ways of working and issues which we may then be faced with.

In order to confront the issues involved in creating and maintaining handicapping conditions in the education of children with severe learning difficulties, we have had to untangle the rhetoric and expose the guises of discrimination. We have also had to question our own beliefs and values and openly criticise ourselves, our colleagues and our chosen profession. By focusing on teaching practice in the education of these children we are asking fellow teachers to examine their own role in creating and maintaining handicapping conditions.

Change at the level of teacher-pupil relationships can be achieved now. It can act as a catalyst for change at other levels of action. It is only through personal changes of attitude and response towards children with severe learning difficulties and mentally handicapped people that handicapping conditions can be removed, disability circumvented, and all people seen as people first who all have abilities as well as disabilities. It is individuals' actions that create change at all levels:

If I blame an evil world, a stupid system, blind teachers, or man's obvious imperfections, I may be right. But if it means I do not have to change, I contribute to the evil. You and I are all that is needed to

147

> change the world. Our necessary confrontation
> is not social. It is personal. The battle is
> not against society but with ourselves
> (B. Blatt, quoted in Williams and Shoultz
> 1982, p. 125).

Group action against structures at a political
level only develops from individual commitment.

BIBLIOGRAPHY

APPLE, M. (1982) Education and Power, Routledge and
    Kegan Paul, London.
ASHEM, B. and POSER, E. (1973) Adaptive Learning
    and Behaviour Modification with Children,
    Pergamon, Oxford.
AXELROD, S. (1977) Behaviour Modification for the
    Classroom Teacher, McGraw-Hill, New York.
BART, D. (1984) "Differential Diagnosis of Special
    Education: Managing Social Pathology as
    Individual Disability", in L. Barton and S.
    Tomlinson, (eds.), Special Education and
    Social Interests, Croom Helm, London.
BARTON, L. and TOMLINSON, S. (eds.), (1981) Special
    Education: Policies, Practices and Social
    Issues, Harper and Row, London.
BARTON, L. and TOMLINSON, S. (eds.), (1984) Special
    Education and Social Interests, Croom Helm,
    London.
BENDER, M. and VALLETUTTI, P. (1976) Teaching The
    Moderately and Severely Handicapped:
    Curriculum Objectives, Strategies and
    Activities, Vol.1 and Vol. II, University Park
    Press, Baltimore, Maryland.
BERCOVICI, S. (1983) Barriers to Normalisation -
    The Restrictive Management of Retarded
    Persons, University Park Press, Baltimore,
    Maryland.
BERESFORD, P., BOOTH, T., CROFT, S. and TUCKWELL,
    P. (1982) "An ESN(S) School and the Labour
    Market", in T. Booth and J. Statham (eds.),
    The Nature of Special Education, Croom Helm,
    London, 230-242.
BLENKIN, G. and KELLY, A. (eds.) (1983) The Primary
    Curriculum in Action, Harper and Row, London.
BOGDAN, R. and KUGELMASS, J. (1984) "Case Studies
    of Mainstreaming: A Symbolic Interactionist
    Approach to Special Schooling" in L. Barton
    and S. Tomlinson (eds.), Special Education and
    Social Interests, Croom Helm, London, 173-191.
BOOTH, T. (1978) "From Normal Baby to Handicapped
    Child", Sociology, 12, (2), 203-222.
BOOTH, T. and STATHAM, J. (eds.), (1982) The Nature
    of Special Education, Croom Helm, London.
BRANDON, D. and RIDLEY, J. (1983) Beginning to
    Listen, a study of the views of residents
    living in a hostel for mentally handicapped
    people, MIND publications, London.
BRECHIN, A., LIDDIARD, P. and SWAIN, J. (eds.),
    (1981) Handicap in a Social World, Hodder and
    Stoughton, London.
BRENNAN, W. (1973) "What training do teachers

require", in The Education of Mentally Handicapped Children, Education and Training Series No. 1, NSMHC, London, 20-25.

BRENNAN, W. (1979) Curricular Needs for Slow Learners, report of the Schools Council Curricular Needs of Slow Learning Pupils' Project, Schools Council Working Paper, 63, Evans/Methuen Educational, London.

BROST, M., JOHNSON, T., WAGNER, L. and DEPREY, R. (1982) Getting to Know You: one approach to service assessment and planning for individuals with disabilities, Wisconsin Council on Developmental Disabilities.

CHAVERT, L. (1979) "Aspects of the curriculum for the child with severe learning difficulties", Apex, 7, (3), 98.

CHILDRIGHT (1983) Childrens' Charters 1, 11-14, Childrens' Legal Centre.

CLARKE, A.M. and CLARKE, A.D.B. (eds.), (1974) Mental Deficiency - The Changing Outlook, Methuen, London.

CRAWFORD, N. (ed.) (1980) Curriculum Planning for the E.S.N.(S) Child, Vol. 1, British Institute of Mental Handicap, Kidderminster.

CRAWLEY, B. (1983) Self Advocacy Manual, Habilitation Technology Project, Paper No. 49, Hester Adrian Research Centre, Manchester University, Manchester.

CUNNINGHAM, C. (1974) "The relevance of normal educational theory and practice for the mentally retarded", in J. Tizard (ed.), Mental Retardation: Concepts of Education and Research, Butterworth, London, 47-55.

DEPARTMENT OF EDUCATION AND SCIENCE (1975) Educating Mentally Handicapped Children, Education Pamphlet No. 60, HMSO, London.
(1980) Special Needs in Education, Cmnd 7996, (White Paper), HMSO, London.
(1981) Circular 6/81, HMSO, London.
(1983a) Statutory Instruments, The Education (Special Educational Needs) Regulations, HMSO, London.
(1983b) Assessments and Statements of Special Educational Needs, Circular 1/83, HMSO, London.
(1984a) Form 7M Special Schools (Other Than Hospital Schools), Return for the Educational year 1983/84, HMSO, London.
(1984b) The Organisation and content of the Curriculum: Special Schools, A Note by the DES and Welsh Office, HMSO, London.

DICKENS, P. (1984) "Evaluating services for people who are mentally handicapped, using PASS", Mental Handicap, 12, (3), 102-103.

EDUCATION (Handicapped Children) ACT 1970, HMSO, London.

EDUCATION ACT 1980, HMSO, London.

EDUCATION ACT (Children with Special Educational Needs) 1981, HMSO, London.

EDY (1978) Education of the Developmentally Young Project, Hester Adrian Research Centre, University of Manchester, Manchester.

EUROPEAN CONVENTION (1965) European Convention on Human Rights.

FARBER, B. (1968) Mental Retardation: Its Social Context and Social Consequences, Houghton Mifflin, Boston.

FINKELSTEIN, V. (1980) Attitudes and Disabled People: issues for discussion, Monograph No. 5, World Rehabilitation Fund Inc., New York.

FOXEN, T. (ed.), (1978) Education of the Developmentally Young (EDY) Project, Hester Adrian Research Centre, University of Manchester, Manchester.

FREIRE, P. (1970) "Pedagogy of the Oppressed", in M. Golby et al. (eds.), 1975, Curriculum Design, Croom Helm, London. 138-149.

FURNEAUX, B. (1984) "Keeping the balance right", Special Education: Forward Trends, 11, (2), 15-16.

GARDNER, J., MURPHY, J. and CRAWFORD, N. (1983) The Skills Analysis Model - an effective curriculum for children with severe learning difficulties, British Institute of Mental Handicap, Kidderminster.

GODDARD, A. (1983) "Processes in Special Education" in G. Blenkin and A. KELLY, (eds.), Primary Curriculum in Action, Harper and Row, London, 248-278.

GOLBY, M., GREENWALD, J. and WEST, R. (eds.),(1975) Curriculum Design, Croom Helm, London/ The Open University Press.

GOODE, D. (1984) "Socially produced identities, intimacy and the problem of competence among the retarded", in L. Barton and S. Tomlinson, (eds.), Special Education and Social Interests, Croom Helm, London, 228-248.

GUNZBERG, H. (1966) Progress Assessment Charts, National Association of Mental Health, London.

GUNZBERG, H. (ed.), (1974a) Experiments in the Rehabilitation of the Mentally Handicapped, Butterworth, London.

GUNZBERG, H. (1974b) "The education of the mentally handicapped child" in A. M. Clarke and A.D.B. Clarke, (eds.), Mental Deficiency, The Changing Outlook, Methuen, London, 628-652.

HEATHCOTE, D. (1981) "Drama and the mentally handicapped", in G. Lord (ed.), The Arts and Disabilities: A Creative Response to Social Handicap, MacDonald Publications Ltd., Edinburgh, 32-37.

HERON, A. and MYERS, M. (1983) Intellectual Impairment - The Battle Against Handicap, Academic Press, London.

HIRST, P. and PETERS, R. (1970) The Logic of Education, Routledge and Kegan Paul, London.

HUGHES, J. (1975) "The educational needs of the mentally handicapped", Educational Research, 17, (3), 228-233.

ILLICH, I. (ed.), (1977) The Disabling Professions, Marion Boyars, London.

INDEPENDENT DEVELOPMENT COUNCIL FOR PEOPLE WITH MENTAL HANDICAP (1984) Next Steps: and independent review of progress, problems and priorities in the development of services for people with mental handicap, I.D.C., London.

JAY REPORT, (1979) Report of the Committee of Enquiry into Mental Handicap Nursing and Care, Cmnd 7468, HMSO, London.

JEFFREE, D., and CHESELDINE, S. (1982)Pathways to Independence, Hodder and Stoughton, London.

KIERNAN, C. (1974) 'Experimental Investigation of the Curriculum for the Profoundly Mentally Retarded' in J. Tizard, (ed.), Mental Retardation - Concepts of Education and Research, Butterworth, London, 57-79.

KIERNAN, C., and WOODFORD, F. (eds.), (1975) Behaviour Modification With the Severely Retarded, IRMH Study Group 8, Associated Scientific Publishers, Amsterdam.

KIERNAN, C., and JONES, M. (1977) Behaviour Assessment Battery, National Foundation for Educational Research, (NFER) - Nelson, Windsor.

KIERNAN, C., JORDAN, R. and SAUNDERS, C. (1978) Starting Off - establishing play and communication in the handicapped child, Souvenir Press (E & A) Ltd., London.

KIERNAN, C. (1980) "General Principles" in N. Crawford, (ed.), Curriculum Planning for ESN(S) Children Vol.1, British Institute of Mental Handicap, Kidderminster.

KIERNAN, C. (1981) Analysis of Programmes for

Teaching, Globe Education/Macmillan Education,
London.
KUGEL, R. and WOLFENSBERGER, W. (eds.), (1969)
Changing Patterns in Residential Services for
the Mentally Retarded, President's Committee
on Mental Retardation, Washington.
LEEMING, K., SWANN, W., COUPE, J. and MITTLER, P.
(1979) Teaching Language and Communication to
the Mentally Handicapped, Evans/Methuen
Educational for the Schools Council, London.
LISHMAN, J. (1981) "Editorial" in S. Reinach (ed.)
Research Highlights No. 2 "Normalisation",
Dept. of Social Work, University of Aberdeen,
Aberdeen, 7-9.
LORD, G. (ed.), (1981) The Arts and Disabilities:
a creative response to social handicap, Mac-
Donald Printers Ltd. , Edinburgh.
McCONKEY, R. (1981) "Education Without
Understanding?", Special Education: Forward
Trends, 8, (3), 8-10.
McKNIGHT, J. (1977) "Professionalised service and
disabling help" in A. Brechin et al., Handicap
in a Social World, Hodder and Stoughton,
Sevenoaks, Kent, 24-33.
McMASTER, J. (1973) Towards an Educational Theory
for the Mentally Handicapped, Edward Arnold,
London.
MITTLER, P. (1981) "Training for the 21st century",
Special Education: Forward Trends, 8,(2),
8-11.
MUNCEY, J. and AINSCOW, M. (1983) "Launching SNAP
in Coventry", Special Education: Forward
Trends,10, (3), 8-12.
PERKINS, E., TAYLOR, P. and CAPIE, A. (1976)
Developmental Checklist (Helping the
Retarded), British Institute of Mental Handi-
cap, Kidderminster.
POTEET, J. (1973) Behaviour Modification - a
practical guide for teachers, University of
London Press, London.
RAMP, E. and SEMB, G. (1975) Behavioural Analysis
-areas of research and analysis, Prentice
Hall, Engelwood Cliffs, New Jersey.
RAYBOULD, E. and SOLITY, J. (1982) "Teaching with
Precision", Special Education: Forward Trends,
9, (2), 9-13.
REINACH, S. (ed.), (1981) Research Highlights No.
2. 'Normalisation', Dept. of Social Work,
University of Aberdeen, Aberdeen.
ROBERTS, N. (1982) "Training or Teaching - the
teacher's role in mental handicap", Mental

Handicap, 10, (4), 127.

SCULL, A. (1977) Decarceration - Community Treatment and the Deviant: a radical view, Prentice Hall, Engelwood Cliffs, New Jersey.

SERPELL-MORRIS, G. (1982) "Minds of their own - one teacher's philosophy", in T. Booth and J. Statham (eds.) The Nature of Special Education, Croom Helm, London, 176-179.

SHAPIRO, H. (1980) "Society, Ideology and the Reform of Special Education: a study in the limits of educational change", Educational Theory, 30, (3), 211-223.

SHARP, R. and GREEN, A. (1975) Education and Social Control, a study in progressive primary education, Routledge and Kegan Paul, London.

SHEARER, A. (1981) Disability: Whose Handicap?, Basil Blackwell, Oxford.

SHEARER, M. and SHEARER, D. (1972) 'The Portage Project: A model for early childhood education', Exceptional Children, 38, 210-217.

SHERBOURNE, V. (1979) 'Movement and Physical Education', in G. Upton, (ed.) Physical and Creative Activities for the Mentally Handicapped, Cambridge University Press, Cambridge, 15-56.

SIMON, G. (ed.) (1980) Modern Management of Mental Handicap - a manual of practice, MTP Press Limited, Lancaster, England.

SINHA, C. (1981) "The role of psychological research in special education", in W. Swann (ed.), The Practice of Special Education, Basil Blackwell, Oxford, 400-435.

SKILBECK, M. (1973) "The School and Cultural Development", in M. Golby et al., Curriculum Design, Croom Helm, London, 27-35.

SMITH, B., MOORE, Y. and PHILLIPS, C. (1983) "Education with Understanding?" Special Education: Forward Trends, 10, (2), 21-24.

SNELL, M. (ed.), (1978) Systematic Instruction of the Moderately and Severely Handicapped, Charles E. Merrill Publishing Co., Columbus, Ohio.

STAFF OF RECTORY PADDOCK SCHOOL (1981) In Search of a Curriculum - notes on the education of mentally handicapped children, Robin Wren Publications, Kent.

STENHOUSE, L. (1975) An Introduction to Curriculum Research and Development, Heinemann, London.

STEVENS, M. (1976) The Educational and Social Needs of Children with Severe Handicap, (2nd edn.), Edward Arnold, London.

STEVENS, M. (1978) Observe - Then Teach, (2nd
    edn.), Edward Arnold, London.
SWANN, W. (ed.) (1981) The Practice of Special
    Education, Basil Blackwell, Oxford.
THE CAMPAIGN FOR MENTALLY HANDICAPPED PEOPLE - CMH
    (1984) Newsletters, Nos. 35, 37, 38, 39.
THE NORFOLK CAMPAIGN FOR PEOPLE WITH MENTAL
    HANDICAPS (1983) Workshop Report.
THOMAS, D. (1982) The Experience of Handicap,
    Methuen and Co. Ltd., London.
TIZARD, J. (ed.), (1974) Mental Retardation -
    Concepts of Education and Research, Butter-
    worth, London.
TOMLINSON, S. (1981) Educational Subnormality, A
    study in Decision-making, Routledge and Kegan
    Paul, London.
TOMLINSON, S. (1982) A Sociology of Special
    Education, Routledge and Kegan Paul, London.
TOPLISS, E. (1982) Social Responses to Handicap,
    Longman, London.
TYNE, A. (1981) 'The impact of the Normalisation
    Principle on Services for the Mentally Handi-
    capped in the United Kingdom', in S. Reinach
    (ed.) Research Highlights No. 2. 'Normalisa-
    tion', Dept. of Social Work,   University
    of Aberdeen, Aberdeen, 23-34.
UNITED NATIONS (1948) Universal Declaration of
    Human Rights.
UNITED NATIONS (1959) Declaration of the Rights of
    the Child.
UNITED NATIONS (1971) Declaration of the Rights of
    Mentally Retarded Persons.
UNITED NATIONS (1975) Declaration on the Rights of
    Disabled Persons.
UPTON, G. (ed.) (1979) Physical and Creative
    Activities for the Mentally Handicapped, Cam-
    bridge University Press, Cambridge.
VARGAS, J. (1977) Behavioural Psychology for
    Teachers, Harper and Row, New York.
WALKER, A. and TOWNSEND, P. (eds.), (1981)
    Disability in Britain - A Manifesto of Rights,
    Martin Robertson and Company Ltd., Oxford.
WARNOCK REPORT (1978) Special Educational Needs,
    Report of the Committee of Enquiry into the
    Education of Handicapped Children and Young
    People, Cmnd 7212, HMSO, London.
WEDELL, K. (1975) Orientations in Special
    Education, Wiley, New York.
WELTON, J., WEDELL, K. and VORHAUS, G. (1982)
    Meeting Special Educational Needs - The 1981
    Education Act and its Implications, Bedford

Way Papers, 12, Institute of Education, University of London, London.

WERTHEIMER, A. (1981) "People with Mental Handicaps", in A. Walker and P. Townsend (eds.), Disability in Britain - A Manifesto of Rights, Martin Robertson, Oxford, 156-174.

WHALEY, D. and MALOTT,R. (1971) Elementary Principles of Behaviour, Prentice Hall Inc., Engelwood Cliffs, New Jersey.

WHELAN, E. and SPEAKE, B. (1979) Learning to Cope, Souvenir Press, London.

WHELAN, E., SPEAKE, B. and STRICKLAND, T. (1984) "The Copewell Curriculum: development, content and use", in A. Dean and S. Hegarty (eds.), Learning for Independence: post 16 educational provision for people with severe learning difficulties, Special Needs Document, Further Education Unit, London.

WILLIAMS, P. and SHOULTZ, B. (1982) We Can Speak for Ourselves, Souvenir Press Ltd., London.

WILLIAMS, R. (1961) "The Long Revolution", in M. Golby et al. (eds.), Curriculum Design, Croom Helm, London, 94-99.

WILSON, J. and COWELL, B. (1984) "How should we define handicap?", Special Education: Forward Trends, 11, (2), 33-35.

WOLFENSBERGER, W. (1969) "The origin and nature of our institutional models", in R. Kugel and W. Wolfensberger (eds.), Changing Patterns in Residential Services for the Mentally Retarded, President's Committee on Mental Retardation, Washington, 59-171.

WOLFENSBERGER, W. and THOMAS, S. (1981) "The principle of normalisation in human services: A brief overview", in S. Reinach (ed.), Research Highlights No. 2. 'Normalisation', Dept. of Social Work, University of Aberdeen, Aberdeen, 10-22.